Neuroqueer Heresies

NOTES ON THE NEURODIVERSITY PARADIGM, AUTISTIC EMPOWERMENT, AND POSTNORMAL POSSIBILITIES

NICK WALKER

AUTON
OMOUS
PRESS

Weird Books for Weird People

2021

Autonomous Press is an independent publisher focusing on works about neurodivergence, queerness, and the various ways they can intersect with each other and with other aspects of identity and lived experience. We are a partnership including writers, poets, artists, musicians, community scholars, and professors. Each partner takes on a share of the work of managing the press and production, and all of our workers are co-owners.

Cover design by Casandra Johns, www.houseofhands.net

ISBN: 978-1-945955-26-6
EISBN: 978-1-945955-27-3

About the Author

Nick Walker is a queer, transgender, flamingly autistic writer and educator best known for her foundational work on the neurodiversity paradigm, her development of the term *neuroqueer* and the concept of neuroqueering, and her contributions to fostering the emergent genre of neuroqueer speculative fiction. She is a professor of psychology at California Institute of Integral Studies, and senior instructor at the Aiki Arts Center in Berkeley.

Dr. Walker is co-founder and Managing Editor of the worker-owned indie publishing house Autonomous Press, and has co-edited and contributed to multiple volumes of the annual *Spoon Knife* neuroqueer lit anthology published by Autonomous Press' Neuro-Queer Books imprint.

Along with her co-writer Andrew M. Reichart and artist Mike Bennewitz, Dr. Walker is part of the creative team behind the urban fantasy webcomic *Weird Luck*.

Website: neuroqueer.com
Webcomic: weirdluck.net
Twitter: @WalkerSensei
Facebook: facebook.com/nickwalkersensei

This book is for all the weird kids.

Contents

PART II: AUTISTIC EMPOWERMENT

PART III: POSTNORMAL POSSIBILITIES

What's in This Book, and How It Came to Be

When I first got involved in online autistic communities back in 2003, the word *neurodiversity* had already been around for a little while. Very few non-autistic folks had heard of it yet, but autistic rights activists were having some exciting conversations about the word's implications. Over the next dozen years or so, through my participation in these conversations and through my published writings, I had the honor of contributing in some small way to the emergence of a new cultural paradigm. I took to calling it the *neurodiversity paradigm*, a name which has caught on in some circles.

While the myriad conversations that shaped the neurodiversity paradigm were unfolding, I finished my undergraduate degree and then my master's degree, and began my doctoral studies. In the papers I wrote for my grad school classes, I explored the phenomenon of neurodiversity and the ways it interconnected with other phenomena like embodiment and gender. In one of those papers, in 2008, I coined the term *neuroqueer*, which became central to my work and eventually became meaningful to a surprising number of other people, too.

In 2013 I created the website *Neurocosmopolitanism* as a public repository for my short essays on autism and the neurodiversity paradigm. Some of those essays ended up having a lasting influence on neurodiversity-related discourse and on the emergent field of Neurodiversity Studies. By the Fall of 2016 I'd drifted away from producing such essays, to focus on finishing my doctoral dissertation and then on writing speculative fiction, comics, and the occasional academic book chapter. I left the essays sitting on the *Neurocosmopolitanism* site until I replaced that whole site with my current site, *Neuroqueer*. For several years now, fans of my online writings—a wildly diverse bunch ranging from widely-published scholars to queer neurodivergent teens—have been reaching out to ask me when the heck I'm going to put my work on neurodiversity and neuroqueerness into a book. And, hey, look, I've finally gone and done it.

The various short chapters that make up this book come in three different flavors: old stuff (most of which was written between 2012 and 2016 and appeared on the *Neurocosmopolitanism* site at one time or another), new commentary on the old stuff, and brand new essays written for this book in the Summer of 2021. I couldn't resist making the occasional edit to some of the older material. Where the wording of a piece in this book differs from another version that appears elsewhere, the version in this book should be regarded as the definitive one for purposes of citation.

The material in this book doesn't appear in the order in which I wrote it. Instead, I've arranged the chapters in an order intended to make the book as coherent as possible. At the beginning of each piece, though, you'll find a note that mentions what year the piece was originally written. Where something I say in a newer piece seems to contradict something I say in an older piece, the newer piece takes precedence and should be considered a better representation of my present understanding. I've learned and grown a great deal over the past decade, and my views have evolved and mutated. By the time you read this book, they'll probably have mutated even further.

The book is divided into three parts:

> *Part I, The Neurodiversity Paradigm*, introduces the neuro-diversity paradigm and some of the key concepts associated with it. This part begins with two of my older and more widely-cited pieces, "Throw Away the Master's Tools: Liberating Ourselves from the Pathology Paradigm" and "Neurodiversity: Some Basic Terms & Definitions" (plus some history and new commentary on those pieces), and then moves on to new material on neurodiversity, the nature of neurotypicality and neurodivergence, the social model of disability, and neurocosmopolitanism.

> *Part II, Autistic Empowerment*, consists of pieces that are specifically focused on autism. Most of the material in Part II was written between 2012 and 2017, but there's also some newer stuff.

> *Part III, Postnormal Possibilities*, consists of my 2015 piece "Neuroqueer: An Introduction," some new commentary on that piece, and a new in-depth discussion of Neuroqueer Theory.

I hope you'll find something, somewhere in all this, that expands your perspective and your sense of possibility.

Nick Walker
Summer 2021
Berkeley, CA

PART I:
THE NEURODIVERSITY PARADIGM

"Homogeneity lacks genius."

Edgar Morin

The Story Behind "Throw Away the Master's Tools"

Back in the early 1990s, a growing number of autistic folks began connecting with one another through the internet and co-creating autistic community, autistic culture, and an autistic rights movement. The autistic rights movement emerged in response to the fact that autism-related discourse and praxis is dominated by what I've termed a *pathology paradigm*, in which autism is framed as a form of medical pathology—a "disorder" or "condition"—and the fact that this pathology paradigm consistently results in autistic people being stigmatized, dehumanized, abused, harmed, and traumatized by professionals and often by their own families.

If we look at the ways in which different historically oppressed groups are oppressed, we can see that the particulars are different for each group but that there are recurring patterns. For instance, the stereotypes projected onto two different groups might be vastly different, but there are consistent patterns in the way that stereotypes get propagated and in the role that stereotyping plays in dehumanizing and disenfranchising members of an oppressed group. An understanding developed among autistic activists that autistics were an oppressed minority group whose oppression in some ways follows similar patterns to those experienced by other historically oppressed groups.

As discussions of these matters unfolded within autistic spaces, new vocabularies had to emerge in order to express new ways of thinking about things. A new conceptual framework was slowly beginning to emerge, and by the late 1990s a crucial piece of this framework's vocabulary had been provided by the emergence of the term *neurodiversity*. Implicit in this juicy new word was an idea that the discourse in the autistic community had been groping its way toward all along: the idea that just as humanity is ethnically diverse and diverse in terms of gender and myriad other qualities, humanity is also neurocognitively diverse. Just as there are ethnic minority groups and gender minority groups, there are neurocognitive minority groups, and that's what autistic people are.

New terms and concepts didn't propagate quite as quickly in those days before the advent of massive social media platforms. In 2003, when I first stepped into the world of online autistic discourse, the term neurodiversity had caught on within some autistic activist circles but was far from widespread. Even those who'd known the word for a few years were still in the early stages of working to grasp and articulate its implications. No one had even coined the obvious corollary term *neurominority* yet; I ended up coining that one myself, in 2004, because it was useful for talking about the sort of things I was trying to talk about at the time (which I suppose is the reason most new words get coined).

The dominant cultural perspective on autism and autistic lives, and the perspective that was developing among those autistic thinkers and activists who were exploring the concept of neurodiversity and its implications, were based in fundamentally different sets of implicit values, goals, and understandings of reality—in other words, in different paradigms. By 2010, I'd started referring to these two contrasting paradigms as the *pathology paradigm* and the *neurodiversity paradigm*—and in the ongoing conversations within what was now being called the Neurodiversity Movement, I'd begun attempting to articulate the nature of these two paradigms and the core distinctions between them.

In 2011, I was invited to contribute to a new book of autistic activist writings. It wasn't the first anthology featuring autistic voices (for example, *Aquamarine Blue 5*, collecting personal accounts of being autistic in college, came out in 2002, and *Ask and Tell*, an early book on self-advocacy skills for autistics, came out in 2004), but it was the first book focused specifically on radical autistic activist voices—the first book in which all of the authors were at least to some degree on board with the emerging neurodiversity paradigm, and were openly and strongly critical of various aspects of the pathology paradigm.

I offered to contribute what I felt was most needed in the discourse at the time: an essay which would define the pathology paradigm, introduce and define the neurodiversity paradigm, and discuss what it meant to make the shift from the pathology paradigm to the neurodiversity paradigm and why such a shift was essential to autistic well-being. I'd been addressing these topics for a while in online discussions, but I'd never before tried to put it all together into a single cohesive piece that aimed to introduce these ideas to new readers in an accessible way.

I called the resulting essay "Throw Away the Master's Tools: Liberating Ourselves from the Pathology Paradigm," and it was my first of writing on autism and the neurodiversity paradigm to be published. That anthology for which I wrote it was published in early 2012, under the title *Loud Hands: Autistic People, Speaking*. It was a groundbreaking book when it came out, though the discourse has advanced so much since then that it's now only of interest for historical purposes.

When I created the *Neurocosmopolitanism* website in 2013, one of the first things I posted on it was a heavily revised version of "Throw Away the Master's Tools." The revisions were badly needed; some of my writing in the original Loud Hands version was embarrassingly clunky. The version that went up on the website (and can now be found on my *Neuroqueer* site) is only about half as clunky, and that's the version that's reprinted here.

This piece was originally written for an autistic audience, so it's specifically addressed to autistic readers and focused on what the shift from the pathology paradigm to the neurodiversity paradigm means in the context of the discourse on autism. Nonetheless, it serves as a good 101-level introduction to the neurodiversity paradigm for anyone, and readers over the past decade have found it a relatively easy matter to extrapolate from my autism-related examples and apply my analysis to the discourses on dyslexia, ADHD, and other pathologized neurocognitive styles.

"Throw Away the Master's Tools" remains one of the more significant things I've written, in terms of its long-term influence on the discourse. It's been widely cited in academic works, and translated into Spanish, French, Portuguese, Russian, and Czech. The conceptions of the pathology paradigm and the neurodiversity paradigm originally articulated in this piece are now integral to the fields of Neurodiversity Studies and Critical Autism Studies, fields which didn't exist yet when I wrote the thing. So much can happen in the blink of a decade.

Throw Away the Master's Tools: Liberating Ourselves from the Pathology Paradigm

When it comes to human neurodiversity, the dominant paradigm in the world today is what I refer to as the *pathology paradigm*. The long-term well-being and empowerment of autistics and members of other neurocognitive minority groups hinges upon our ability to create a paradigm shift—a shift from the pathology paradigm to the *neurodiversity paradigm*. Such a shift must happen internally, within the consciousness of individuals, and must also be propagated in the cultures in which we live.

So what does all that fancy talk mean? What are these paradigms of which I speak, and what does it mean to make a "shift" from one paradigm to another? This piece is an attempt to explain that, in plain language that I hope will make these concepts easily accessible.

What's a Paradigm, and What's a Paradigm Shift?

Even if you haven't encountered it in an academic context, you've probably heard the term *paradigm* before, because it's annoyingly overused by corporate marketers to describe any new development they're trying to get people excited about: *A new paradigm in wireless technology! A new paradigm in sales hyperbole!*

As a great Spanish diplomat once put it, I do not think it means what they think it means.

A paradigm is not just an idea or a method. A paradigm is a set of fundamental assumptions or principles, a mindset or frame of reference that shapes how one thinks about and talks about a given subject. A paradigm shapes the ways in which one interprets information, and determines what sort of questions one asks and how one asks them. A paradigm is a lens through which one views reality.

Perhaps the most simple and well-known example of a paradigm shift comes from the history of astronomy: the shift from the *geocentric paradigm* (which assumes that the Sun and planets revolve around Earth) to the *heliocentric paradigm* (Earth and several other planets revolve around the Sun). At the time this shift began, many generations of astronomers had already recorded extensive observations of the movements of planets. But now all their measurements meant something different. All the information had to be reinterpreted from an entirely new perspective. It wasn't just that questions had new answers—the questions themselves were different. Questions like "What is the path of Mercury's orbit around Earth?" went from seeming important to being outright nonsense, while other questions, that had never been asked because they would have seemed like nonsense under the old paradigm, suddenly became meaningful.

That's a true paradigm shift: a shift in our fundamental assumptions; a radical shift in perspective that requires us to redefine our terms, recalibrate our language, rephrase our questions, reinterpret our data, and completely rethink our basic concepts and approaches.

The Pathology Paradigm

A paradigm can often be boiled down to a few basic, general principles, although those principles tend to be far-reaching in their implications and consequences. The principles of a widely dominant sociocultural paradigm like the pathology paradigm usually take the form of *assumptions*—that is, they're so widely taken-for-granted that most people never consciously reflect upon them or articulate them (and sometimes it can be a disturbing revelation to hear them plainly articulated). The pathology paradigm ultimately boils down to just two fundamental assumptions:

1. There is one "right," "normal," or "healthy" way for human brains and human minds to be configured and to function (or one relatively narrow "normal" range into which the configuration and functioning of human brains and minds ought to fall).

2. If your neurological configuration and functioning (and, as a result, your ways of thinking and behaving) diverge substantially from the dominant standard of "normal," then there is Something Wrong With You.

It is these two assumptions that define the pathology paradigm. Different groups and individuals build upon these assumptions in very different ways, with varying degrees of rationality, absurdity, fearfulness, or compassion—but as long as they share those two basic assumptions, they're still operating within the pathology paradigm (just as ancient Mayan astronomers and 13th Century Islamic astronomers had vastly different conceptions of the cosmos, yet both operated within the geocentric paradigm).

The psychiatric establishment that classifies autism as a "disorder";

the "autism charity" that calls autism a "global health crisis"; autism researchers who keep coming up with new theories of "causation"; scientifically illiterate wing nuts who believe that autism is some form of "poisoning"; anyone who speaks of autism using medicalized language like "symptom," "treatment," or "epidemic"; the mother who thinks that the best way to help her autistic child is to subject him to Behaviorist "interventions" intended to train him to act like a "normal" child; the "inspiring" autistic celebrity who advises other autistics that the secret to success is to try harder to conform to the social demands of non-autistics... *all* of these groups and individuals are operating within the pathology paradigm, regardless of their intentions or how much they might disagree with one another on various points.

The Neurodiversity Paradigm

Here's how I'd articulate the fundamental principles of the neurodiversity paradigm:

1. Neurodiversity—the diversity among minds—is a natural, healthy, and valuable form of human diversity.

2. There is no "normal" or "right" style of human mind, any more than there is one "normal" or "right" ethnicity, gender, or culture.

3. The social dynamics that manifest in regard to neurodiversity are similar to the social dynamics that manifest in regard to other forms of human diversity (e.g., diversity of race, culture, gender, or sexual orientation). These dynamics in-

clude the dynamics of social power relations—the dynamics of social inequality, privilege, and oppression—as well as the dynamics by which diversity, when embraced, acts as a source of creative potential within a group or society.

The Master's Tools Will Never Dismantle the Master's House

At an international feminist conference in 1979, the poet Audre Lorde delivered a speech entitled "The Master's Tools Will Never Dismantle the Master's House." In that speech, Lorde, a Black lesbian from a working-class immigrant family, castigated her almost entirely white and affluent audience for remaining rooted in, and continuing to propagate, the fundamental dynamics of the patriarchy: hierarchy, exclusion, racism, classism, homophobia, obliviousness to privilege, failure to embrace diversity. Lorde recognized sexism as being part of a broader, deeply-rooted paradigm that dealt with all forms of difference by establishing hierarchies of dominance, and she saw that genuine, widespread liberation was impossible as long as feminists continued to operate within this paradigm.

"What does it mean," Lorde said, "when the tools of a racist patriarchy are used to examine the fruits of that same patriarchy? It means that only the most narrow perimeters of change are possible and allowable. [...] For the master's tools will never dismantle the master's house. They may allow us temporarily to beat him at his own game, but they will never enable us to bring about genuine change."

The master's tools will never dismantle the master's house. To work within a system, to play by its rules, inevitably reinforces that system, whether or not that's what you intend. Not only do the master's tools never serve to dismantle the master's house, but any time you try to use the master's tools for *anything,* you somehow end up building another extension of that darned house.

Lorde's warning applies equally well, today, to the autistic community and our fight for empowerment. The assumption that there is Something Wrong With Us is inherently disempowering, and that assumption is absolutely intrinsic to the pathology paradigm. So the "tools" of the pathology paradigm (by which I mean all strategies, goals, or ways of speaking or thinking that explicitly or implicitly buy into the pathology paradigm's assumptions) will never empower us in the long run. Genuine, lasting, widespread empowerment for autistics can only be attained through making and propagating the shift from the pathology paradigm to the neurodiversity paradigm. We must throw away the master's tools.

The Language of Pathology vs. the Language of Diversity

Because the pathology paradigm has been dominant for some time, many people, even many who claim to advocate for the empowerment of autistic people, still habitually use language that's based in the assumptions of that paradigm. The shift from the pathology paradigm to the neurodiversity paradigm calls for a radical shift in language, because the appropriate language for discussing medical problems is quite different from the appropriate language for discussing diversity. The issue of "person-first language" is a good basic example to start with.

If a person has a medical condition, we might say that "she has cancer," or she's "a person with allergies," or "she suffers from ulcers." But when a person is a member of a historically marginalized group, we don't talk about their identity as though it were a disease. We say "she's Black," or "she's a lesbian." We recognize that it would be outrageously inappropriate—and likely to mark us as ignorant or bigoted—if we were to refer to a Black person as "having negroism" or being a "person with negroism," or if we were to say that someone "suffers from homosexuality."

So if we use phrases like "person with autism," or "she has autism," or "families affected by autism," we're using the language of the pathology paradigm—language that implicitly accepts and reinforces the assumption that autism is intrinsically a problem, a Something-Wrong-With-You. In the language of the neurodiversity paradigm, on the other hand, we speak of neurodiversity in the same way we would speak of ethnic or sexual diversity, and we speak of autistics in the same way we would speak of any other social minority group: *I am autistic. I am an autistic. I am an autistic person. There are autistic people in my family.*

These linguistic distinctions might seem trivial, but our language plays a key role in shaping our thoughts, our perceptions, our cultures, and our realities. In the long run, the sort of language that's used to talk about autistics has enormous influence on how society treats us, and on the messages we internalize about ourselves. To describe ourselves in language that reinforces the pathology paradigm is to use the master's tools, in Audre Lorde's metaphor, and thus to imprison ourselves more deeply in the master's house.

I Don't Believe in Normal People

The concept of a "normal brain" or a "normal person" has no more objective scientific validity—and serves no better purpose—than the concept of a "master race." Of all the master's tools (i.e., the dynamics, language, and conceptual frameworks that create and maintain social inequities), the most powerful and insidious is the concept of "normal people." In the context of human diversity (ethnic, cultural, sexual, neurological, or any other sort), to treat one particular group as the "normal" or default group inevitably serves to privilege that group and to marginalize those who don't belong to that group.

The dubious assumption that there's such a thing as a "normal person" lies at the core of the pathology paradigm. The neurodiversity paradigm, on the other hand, does not recognize "normal" as a valid concept when it comes to human diversity.

Most reasonably well-educated people these days already recognize that the concept of "normal" is absurd and meaningless in the context of racial, ethnic, or cultural diversity. The Han Chinese constitute the single largest ethnic group in the world, but it would be ridiculous to claim that this makes Han Chinese the "natural" or "default" human ethnicity. The fact that a randomly-selected human is statistically far more likely to be Han Chinese than Irish does not make a Han Chinese more "normal" than an Irishman (whatever that would even mean).

The most insidious sort of social inequality, the most difficult sort of privilege to challenge, occurs when a dominant group is so deeply established as the "normal" or "default" group that it has no specific name, no label. The members of such a group are simply thought of as "normal people," "healthy people," or just "people"—with the implication that those who aren't members of that group represent deviations from that which is normal and natural, rather than equally natural and legitimate manifestations of human diversity.

For instance, consider the connotations of the statement "Gay people want the same rights as heterosexuals," versus the connotations of the statement "Gay people want the same rights as normal people." Simply by substituting the word *normal* for *heterosexual,* the second statement implicitly accepts and reinforces heterosexual privilege, and relegates gays to an inferior, "abnormal" status.

Now imagine if terms like *heterosexual* and *straight* didn't exist at all. That would put gay rights activists in the position of having to say things like "We want the same rights as normal people"—language that would reinforce their marginal, "abnormal" status and thus undermine their struggle. They'd be stuck using the master's tools. If terms like *heterosexual* and *straight* didn't exist, it would be necessary for gay rights activists to invent them.

This is why an essential early step in the neurodiversity movement was the coining of the term *neurotypical*. *Neurotypical* is to *autistic* as *straight* is to *gay.* The existence of the word *neurotypical* makes it possible to have conversations about topics like neurotypical privilege. *Neurotypical* is a word that allows us to talk about members of the dominant neurological group without implicitly reinforcing that group's privileged position (and our own marginalization) by referring to them as "normal." The word *normal,* used to privilege one sort of human over others, is one of the master's tools, but the word *neurotypical* is one of *our* tools—a tool that we can use *instead of* the master's tool; a tool that *can* help us to dismantle the master's house.

The Vocabulary of Neurodiversity

The word *neurotypical* is an essential piece of the new vocabulary of neurodiversity that's beginning to emerge—that *needs* to emerge, if we are to free ourselves of the disempowering language of the pathology paradigm, and if we are to successfully propagate the neurodiversity paradigm in our own thinking and in the sphere of public discourse.

The word *neurodiversity* itself is of course the most essential piece of this new vocabulary. The essence of the entire paradigm—the understanding of neurological variation as a natural form of human diversity, subject to the same societal dynamics as other forms of diversity—is packed into that one word.

Another useful word is *neurominority.* Neurotypicals are the majority; autistic people and dyslexic people are examples of neurominorities. I'd like to see the term *neurominority* come into more widespread usage, because there's a need for it; there are a lot of topics in the discourse on neurodiversity that are much easier to talk about when one has a good, non-pathologizing word for referring to the various groups of people who aren't neurotypical.

Terms like *neurodiversity, neurotypical,* and *neurominority* allow us to talk and think about neurodiversity in ways that don't implicitly pathologize neurominority individuals. As we cultivate autistic community and interact with other neurominority communities, and as we continue to generate writing and discussion on issues of relevance to us, more new language will emerge. Already, we've generated terms like *stim* and *loud hands* to describe important aspects of the autistic experience. And in my own academic work, my studies of cross-cultural competence (the ability to interact and communicate skillfully with people from multiple cultures) have led me to begin using the term *neurocosmopolitanism,* which I hope will catch on widely.

It's also my hope that the terms *neurodiversity paradigm* and *pathology paradigm* will catch on and come into widespread usage. In the interest of clarity, it's useful to make the distinction between *neurodiversity* (the phenomenon of human neurological diversity) and the *neurodiversity paradigm* (the understanding of neurodiversity as a natural form of human diversity, subject to the same societal dynamics as other forms of diversity). And having a name for the pathology paradigm makes that paradigm much easier to discuss, recognize, challenge, and deconstruct—and eventually dismantle.

Words are tools. And as we recognize that the master's tools will never dismantle the master's house, we are creating our own tools, which can help us not only to dismantle the master's house, but to build a new house in which we can live better, more empowered lives.

Outposts in Your Head

It breaks my heart when so many of the autistic people I meet speak of themselves and think of themselves in the language of the pathology paradigm, and when I see how this disempowers them and keeps them feeling bad about themselves. They've spent their lives listening to the toxic messages spread by proponents of the pathology paradigm, and they've accepted and internalized those messages and now endlessly repeat them in their own heads.

When we recognize that the struggles of neurominorities largely follow the same dynamics as the struggles of other sorts of minority groups, we recognize this self-pathologizing talk as a manifestation of a problem that has plagued members of many minority groups—a phenomenon called *internalized oppression.*

A contemporary of Audre Lorde's, the feminist journalist Sally Kempton, had this to say about internalized oppression: "It's hard to fight an enemy who has outposts in your head."

The task of liberating ourselves from the master's house begins with dismantling the parts of that house that have been built within our own heads. And *that* process begins with throwing away the master's tools so that we stop inadvertently building up the very thing we're trying to dismantle.

Throwing Away the Master's Tools

Once we recognize that the foundation of the pathology paradigm—the fictive concept of "normal people"—is a fundamental element of the master's toolkit, it becomes a lot easier to identify and rid ourselves of the master's tools. All we need to do is take careful stock of our words, concepts, thoughts, beliefs, and worries, and see whether they still make sense if we throw out the concept of "normal," the concept that there's one "right" way for people's brains and minds to function.

Once we've thrown away the concept of "normal," neurotypicals are just members of a majority—not healthier or more "right" than the rest of us, just more common. And autistics are a minority group, no more intrinsically "disordered" than any ethnic minority. When we realize that "normal" is just something a bunch of people made up, when we recognize it as one of the master's tools and toss it out the window, the idea of autism as a "disorder" goes out the window right along with it. Disordered compared to what state of order, exactly, if we refuse to buy into the idea that there's one particular "normal" order to which all minds should conform?

Without the fictive reference point of "normal," functioning labels—"high-functioning autism" and "low-functioning autism"—are also revealed to be absurd fictions. "High-functioning" or "low-functioning" compared to *what?* Who gets to decide what the proper "function" of any individual human should be?

In the pathology paradigm, the neurotypical mind is enthroned as the "normal" ideal against which all other types of minds are measured. "Low-functioning" really means "far from passing for neurotypical, far from being able to do the things that neurotypicals think people should do, and far from being able to thrive in a society created by and for neurotypicals." "High-functioning" means "closer to passing for neurotypical." To describe yourself as "high-functioning" is to use the master's tools, to wall yourself up in the master's house—a house in which neurotypicals are the ideal standard against which you should be measured, a house in which neurotypicals are always at the top, and in which "higher" means "more like them."

If we start from the assumption that neurotypicals are "normal," and autistics are "disordered," then poor connections between neurotypicals and autistics inevitably get blamed on some "defect" or "deficit" in autistics. If an autistic person can't understand a neurotypical, it's because autistics have empathy deficits and impaired communication skills; if a neurotypical can't understand an autistic person, it's because autistics have empathy deficits and poor communication skills. All the frictions and failures of connection between the two groups, and all the difficulties autistics run into in neurotypical society, all get blamed on autism. But when our vision is no longer clouded by the illusion of "normal," we can recognize this double standard for what it is, recognize it as just another manifestation of the sort of privilege and power that dominant majorities so often wield over minorities of any sort.

Life Beyond the Pathology Paradigm

A paradigm shift, as you may recall, requires that all data be reinterpreted through the lens of the new paradigm. If you reject the fundamental premises of the pathology paradigm, and accept the premises of the neurodiversity paradigm, then it turns out that you don't have a disorder after all. And it turns out that maybe you function exactly as you ought to function, and that you just live in a society that isn't yet sufficiently enlightened to effectively accommodate and integrate people who function like you. And that maybe the troubles in your life have not been the result of any inherent wrongness in you. And that your true potential is unknown and is yours to explore. And that maybe you are, in fact, a thing of beauty.

Comments on "Throw Away the Master's Tools"

Re-reading "Throw Away the Master's Tools" in the Summer of 2021, as I put this book together, I was pleasantly surprised at how much of it still holds up reasonably well, a decade after I wrote the original draft.

One thing that I feel is worth emphasizing here is that the pathology paradigm and the neurodiversity paradigm are as fundamentally incompatible as, say, homophobia and the gay rights movement, or misogyny and feminism. In terms of discourse, research, and policy, the pathology paradigm asks, in essence, "What do we do about the problem of these people not being normal," while the neurodiversity paradigm asks, "What do we do about the problem of these people being oppressed, marginalized, and/or poorly served and poorly accommodated by the prevailing culture?"

•

It's also worth noting that the growing popularity of the term *neurodiversity* has led to its widespread appropriation as a buzzword by a lot of individuals and organizations who don't understand its implications and are still very much thinking and operating within the pathology paradigm. It's far too common these days to see some website or article that uses the word *neurodiversity* and then proceeds to talk about autism and/or other forms of neurodivergence in highly pathologizing ways—for example, referring to them as "conditions," promoting the old pathology paradigm stereotypes and canards, or rating autistic people as "high-functioning" or "low-functioning" based on how close they come to passing for neurotypical. So it's important to remember that mere adoption of terminology isn't the same as actually making a meaningful shift in mindset. It's important to keep thinking critically about how neurodiversity-related terms are being used (or misused) in a given context, and whether the underlying premises involved are the premises of the neurodiversity paradigm or of the pathology paradigm.

•

Toward the end of "Throw Away the Master's Tools," I discussed the pathology paradigm terms "high-functioning" and "low-functioning"—terms which assume that neurotypicality represents the "highest" human ideal, and which rate autistic human beings as "higher" or "lower" based on how well they conform to dominant social norms of neurotypical performance. Contemplating this part of the essay now, I'd like to propose that instead of rating human beings as "high-functioning" or "low-functioning," we apply the terms "high-functioning" and "low-functioning" to *societies*, rating the functioning of a society according to the degree to which it succeeds in supporting and furthering the well-being of all of its members—and the degree to which it can accommodate and integrate diversity, and employ diversity as a creative resource, without attempting to reduce or eliminate it and without establishing hierarchies of dominance and oppression.

•

Another thing I wrote toward the end of "Throw Away the Master's Tools" was this:

> If we start from the assumption that neurotypicals are "normal," and autistics are "disordered," then poor connections between neurotypicals and Autistics inevitably get blamed on some "defect" or "deficit" in autistics. If an autistic person can't understand a neurotypical, it's because autistics have empathy deficits and impaired communication skills; if a neurotypical can't understand an autistic person, it's because autistics have empathy deficits and poor communication skills. All the frictions and failures of connection between the two groups, and all the difficulties autistics run into in neurotypical society, all get blamed on autism. But when our vision is no longer clouded by the illusion of "normal," we can recognize this double standard for what it is, recognize it as just another manifestation of the sort of privilege and power that dominant majorities so often wield over minorities of any sort.

It's worth noting here that right around the time I wrote the original version of "Throw Away the Master's Tools," my fellow autistic scholar Damian Milton began writing academic articles focused on the particular phenomenon I described in the above paragraph—the fact that it's harder for people to understand each other when their respective modes of experience and cognition differ significantly, and under the pathology paradigm this mutual gap of understanding is blamed entirely on alleged autistic deficits rather than treated as a mutual communication challenge to be worked on reciprocally. Milton dubbed this double standard the *Double Empathy Problem*, and it's a phenomenon that's now widely recognized and discussed in the field of Critical Autism Studies.

•

Two other things it occurred to me to comment upon and expand upon further as I re-read "Throw Away the Master's Tools" were the definition of *neurodiversity* and the definition of *neurotypical*. But those comments ended up long enough that I turned them into their own separate chapters, "Defining Neurodiversity" and "Defining Neurotypicality & Neurodivergence," which appear a little bit later in this book.

Neurodiversity: Some Basic Terms & Definitions

I originally wrote this piece for the Neurocosmopolitanism website in September of 2014, and these days it lives on the Neuroqueer site. There's not much story behind this one to tell, beyond what's already stated in the opening paragraphs of the piece itself: I created it as a public service because I saw a lot of confused people using neurodiversity-related terms incorrectly. So far, of all the pieces I've written, this is the one that's been most frequently cited in other people's writing—academic and otherwise—and most frequently linked to online.

New paradigms often require a bit of new language, and this is certainly the case with the neurodiversity paradigm. I see many people—scholars, journalists, bloggers, internet commenters, and even people who identify as neurodiversity activists—get confused about the terminology around neurodiversity. Their misunderstanding and incorrect usage of certain terms often results in poor and clumsy communication of their message, and propagation of further confusion (including other confused people imitating their errors). At the very least, incorrect use of terminology can make a writer or speaker appear ignorant, or an unreliable source of information, in the eyes of those who *do* understand the meanings of the terms.

For those of us who seek to propagate and build upon the neurodiversity paradigm—especially those of us who are producing writing on neurodiversity—it's vital that we maintain some basic clarity and consistency of language, for the sake of effective communication among ourselves and with our broader audiences. Clarity of language supports clarity of understanding.

And, as I increasingly find myself in the position of reviewing other people's writing on neurodiversity—grading student papers, reviewing book submissions or submissions to journals, consulting on various projects, or even just deciding which pieces of writing I'm willing to recommend to people—I'm getting tired of running into the same basic errors over and over.

So, as a public service, I've created this list of a few key neurodiversity-related terms, their meanings and proper usage, and the ways in which I most commonly see them *mis*used.

NEURODIVERSITY

What It Means:

Neurodiversity is the diversity of human minds, the infinite variation in neurocognitive functioning within our species.

What It Doesn't Mean:

Neurodiversity is a biological fact. It's *not* a perspective, an approach, a belief, a political position, or a paradigm. That's the *neurodiversity paradigm* (see below), not neurodiversity itself.

Neurodiversity is *not* a political or social activist movement. That's the *Neurodiversity Movement* (see below), not neurodiversity itself.

Neurodiversity is *not* a trait that any individual possesses or can possess. When an individual or group of individuals diverges from the dominant societal standards of "normal" neurocognitive functioning, they don't "have neurodiversity," they're *neurodivergent* (see below).

Example of Correct Usage:

"*Our school offers multiple learning strategies to accommodate the neurodiversity of our student body.*"

Examples of Incorrect Usage:

"*Neurodiversity claims that…*"

This writer is actually trying to talk about either the *neurodiversity paradigm* or the *Neurodiversity Movement*. Neurodiversity, as a biological characteristic of the species, can't "claim" anything, any more than variations in human skin pigmentation can "claim" something.

"*Neurodiversity is a load of nonsense.*"

Really? So human brains and minds don't differ from one another? There's an awful lot of scientific evidence that shows quite plainly that there's considerable variation among human brains. And if we all thought alike, the world would be a very different place indeed. The person who wrote this sentence was probably trying to object to the *neurodiversity paradigm* and/or the positions of the *Neurodiversity Movement,* and has ended up sounding rather silly as a result of failing to distinguish between these things and the phenomenon of neurodiversity itself.

"*My neurodiversity makes it hard for me to cope with school.*" The correct word here would be *neurodivergence*, rather than neurodiversity. An individual, by definition, cannot be "diverse" or "have diversity."

"Autism and dyslexia are forms of neurodiversity."

Nope. Nope, nope, nope. There's no such thing as a "form of neurodiversity." Autism and dyslexia are forms of *neurodivergence*.

NEURODIVERSITY PARADIGM

What It Means:

The neurodiversity paradigm is a specific perspective on neurodiversity—a perspective or approach that boils down to these fundamental principles:

1. Neurodiversity is a natural and valuable form of human diversity.

2. The idea that there is one "normal" or "healthy" type of brain or mind, or one "right" style of neurocognitive functioning, is a culturally constructed fiction, no more valid (and no more conducive to a healthy society or to the overall well-being of humanity) than the idea that there is one "normal" or "right" ethnicity, gender, or culture.

3. The social dynamics that manifest in regard to neurodiversity are similar to the social dynamics that manifest in regard to other forms of human diversity (e.g., diversity of ethnicity, gender, or culture). These dynamics include the dynamics of social power inequalities, and also the dynamics by which diversity, when embraced, acts as a source of creative potential.

What It Doesn't Mean:

The neurodiversity paradigm provides a philosophical foundation for the activism of the *Neurodiversity Movement*, but the two aren't the same. For instance, there are people working on developing inclusive education strategies based on the neurodiversity paradigm, who don't identify as social justice activists or as part of the Neurodiversity Movement.

Example of Correct Usage:

"Those who have embraced the neurodiversity paradigm, and who truly understand it, do not use pathologizing terms like 'disorder' to describe neurocognitive variants like autism."

NEURODIVERSITY MOVEMENT

What It Means:

The *Neurodiversity Movement* is a social justice movement that seeks civil rights, equality, respect, and full societal inclusion for the neurodivergent.

What It Doesn't Mean:

The Neurodiversity Movement is not a single group or organization, is not run by any single group or organization, and has no leader. Like most civil rights movements, the Neurodiversity Movement is made up of a great many individuals, some of them organized into groups of one sort or another. These individuals and groups are quite diverse in their viewpoints, goals, concerns, political positions, affiliations, methods of activism, and interpretations of the neurodiversity paradigm.

The Neurodiversity Movement began within the Autism Rights Movement, and there is still a great deal of overlap between the two movements. But the Neurodiversity Movement and the Autism Rights Movement are not one and the same. The most significant distinction between the two is that the Neurodiversity Movement seeks to be inclusive of all neurominorities, not just autistics. Also, there some who advocate for the rights of autistics but who cannot rightly be considered part of the Neurodiversity Movement because they still consider autism to be a medical pathology or "disorder," a view at odds with the neurodiversity paradigm.

NEURODIVERGENT and NEURODIVERGENCE

What It Means:

Neurodivergent, sometimes abbreviated as *ND*, means having a mind that functions in ways which diverge significantly from the dominant societal standards of "normal."

Neurodivergent is quite a broad term. *Neurodivergence* (the state of being neurodivergent) can be largely or entirely genetic and innate, or it can be largely or entirely produced by brain-altering experience, or some combination of the two. Autism and dyslexia are examples of innate forms of neurodivergence, while alterations in brain functioning caused by such things as trauma, long-term meditation practice, or heavy usage of psychedelic drugs are examples of forms of neurodivergence produced through experience.

A person whose neurocognitive functioning diverges from dominant societal norms in multiple ways—for instance, a person who is autistic, dyslexic, and epileptic—can be described as *multiply neurodivergent*.

Some forms of innate or largely innate neurodivergence, like autism, are intrinsic and pervasive factors in an individual's psyche, personality, and fundamental way of relating to the world. The neurodiversity paradigm rejects the pathologizing of such forms of neurodivergence, and the Neurodiversity Movement opposes attempts to get rid of them.

Other forms of neurodivergence, like epilepsy or the effects of traumatic brain injuries, could be removed from an individual without erasing fundamental aspects of the individual's selfhood, and in many cases the individual would be happy to be rid of such forms of neurodivergence. The neurodiversity paradigm does not reject the pathologizing of these forms of neurodivergence, and the Neurodiversity Movement does not object to consensual attempts to cure them (but still most definitely objects to discrimination against people who have them).

Thus, neurodivergence is not intrinsically positive or negative, desirable or undesirable—it all depends on what sort of neurodivergence one is talking about.

The terms *neurodivergent* and *neurodivergence* were coined in the year 2000 by Kassiane Asasumasu, a multiply neurodivergent neurodiversity activist.

What It Doesn't Mean:

Neurodivergent is not a synonym for *autistic*. There are countless possible ways to be neurodivergent, and being autistic is only one of those ways. There are myriad ways of being neurodivergent that have no resemblance or connection to autism whatsoever. Never, ever use *neurodivergent* as a euphemism for *autistic*. If you mean that someone is autistic, say they're autistic. It's not a dirty word.

Examples of Correct Usage:

"*Our school aims to be inclusive of students who are Autistic, dyslexic, or otherwise neurodivergent, though there are some types of neurodivergence that we're still seeking ways to accommodate.*"

"*This group is for people who identify as both queer and ND (neurodivergent).*"

NEUROTYPICAL, or NT

What It Means:

Neurotypical, often abbreviated as *NT*, means having a style of neurocognitive functioning that falls within the dominant societal standards of "normal."

Neurotypical can be used as either an adjective ("He's neurotypical") or a noun ("He's a neurotypical").

Neurotypical is the opposite of *neurodivergent*. Neurotypicality is the way-of-being from which neurodivergent people diverge. Neurotypical bears the same sort of relationship to neurodivergent that *straight* bears to *queer*.

What It Doesn't Mean:

Neurotypical is *not* synonymous with *non-autistic*.

Neurotypical is the opposite of neurodivergent, not the opposite of autistic. Autism is only one of many forms of neurodivergence, so there are many, many people who are neither neurotypical nor autistic. Using neurotypical to mean non-autistic is like using "white" to mean "not black."

Also, neurotypical is not a derogatory word, and has no intrinsic negative connotation. Of course, sometimes people use the word in the context of criticizing the behavior of neurotypicals, but that doesn't make it an intrinsically negative word. A lot of people criticize the behavior of men, too, but that doesn't make "man" an intrinsically derogatory word.

Examples of Correct Usage:

"*If the primary language of the society in which you were born is well-suited to the purpose of describing your sensory experiences, your needs, and your thought processes, you may have neurotypical privilege.*"

"*My sister is NT, but after growing up with an Autistic father and brother, she's quite at ease with other people's neurodivergence.*"

Example of Incorrect Usage:

"*Is your daughter Autistic or neurotypical?*"

This isn't a well-worded question because there are other possibilities. The daughter in question might be non-autistic, but might also not qualify as neurotypical—she might, for instance, be dyslexic or have Down Syndrome.

NEUROMINORITY

What It Means:

A *neurominority* is a population of neurodivergent people about whom all of the following are true:

1. They all share a similar form of neurodivergence.

2. The form of neurodivergence they share is one of those forms that is largely innate and that is inseparable from who they are, constituting an intrinsic and pervasive factor in their psyches, personalities, and fundamental ways of relating to the world.

3. The form of neurodivergence they share is one to which the neurotypical majority tends to respond with some degree of prejudice, misunderstanding, discrimination, and/or oppression (generally facilitated by classifying that form of neurodivergence as a medical pathology).

Some examples of neurominority groups include autistic people, dyslexic people, and people with Down Syndrome.

It's also possible to be neurodivergent *without* being a member of a neurominority group. Examples include people with acquired traumatic brain injuries, and people who have altered their own neurocognitive functioning through extensive use of psychedelic drugs.

The word *neurominority* can function as either a noun (as in, "autistics are a neurominority") or an adjective (as in, "autistics are a neurominority group").

NEURODIVERSE

What It Means:

A group of people is *neurodiverse* if one or more members of the group differ substantially from other members, in terms of their neurocognitive functioning.

Or, to phrase it another way, a neurodiverse group is a group in which multiple neurocognitive styles are represented.

Thus, a family, the faculty or student body of a school, the population of a town, or the cast of characters of a TV show would be neurodiverse if some members had different neurocognitive styles from other members—for instance, if some members were neurotypical while others were autistic.

What It Doesn't Mean:

Many people mistakenly use *neurodiverse* where the correct word would be *neurodivergent*. Of all the errors that people make in writing and speaking about neurodiversity, the misuse of *neurodiverse* to mean *neurodivergent* is by far the most common.

There is no such thing as a "neurodiverse individual." The correct term is "*neurodivergent* individual." An individual can diverge, but *an individual cannot be diverse.*

Neurodiverse does *not* mean "non-neurotypical." The opposite of *neurotypical* is *neurodivergent*, not neurodiverse. Neurodiverse cannot be used to mean "non-neurotypical," because neurotypical people, like all other human beings, are part of the spectrum of human neurodiversity. The opposite of neurodiverse would be *neurohomogenous* (meaning "composed of people who are all neurocognitively similar to one another").

To refer to neurominority groups or neurodivergent individuals as "neurodiverse" is incorrect grammatically, because *diverse* doesn't mean *different from the majority*, it means *made up of multiple different types*. So an individual can never be diverse, by definition. And a group where everyone is neurodivergent in more or less the same way (e.g., a group composed entirely of autistic people) wouldn't be "neurodiverse," either.

The *only* appropriate and grammatically correct use of the term neurodiverse is when it's used to describe a group of people whose members differ neurocognitively *from each other*. In other words, a classroom where everyone is autistic is not neurodiverse, but a classroom where some students are neurotypical and some aren't is neurodiverse.

Humanity is neurodiverse, just as humanity is racially, ethnically, and culturally diverse. By definition, *no* human being falls outside of the spectrum of human neurodiversity, just as no human being falls outside of the spectrum of human racial, ethnic, and cultural diversity.

In addition to being incorrect, it's also *oppressive* to misuse the word "diverse" to mean "minority," because this misuse of "diverse" is based in the intrinsically oppressive assumption that there's a default "normal" way of being and that "diversity" is about adding non-normative individuals into the "normal" default environment. This is the assumption that allows tokenization to pass for "diversity" in corporations, schools, and other social institutions.

We can see this same oppressive misuse of the word "diverse" in the discourse of racists who use the term "diverse" as a euphemism for "non-white." This usage seeks to twist the definition of the word "diverse" to mean "not part of the privileged in-group." Again, that's not what the word means, and misusing it in that particular way serves to reinforce a racist mindset in which white people are seen as intrinsically separate from the rest of humanity, rather than as just another part of the spectrum of human ethnic diversity.

It is the same with the misuse of the term neurodiverse to mean "non-neurotypical." To describe an autistic, dyslexic, or otherwise neurodivergent person as a "neurodiverse individual" is not merely an incorrect usage of the word "diverse"—it also serves to reinforce an ableist mindset in which neurotypical people are seen as intrinsically separate from the rest of humanity, rather than as just another part of the spectrum of human neurodiversity.

In summary, then: misusing the term *neurodiverse* to mean *neurodivergent* (i.e., non-neurotypical) is not only plain old bad grammar, it also subtly reinforces ableism and undercuts the fundamental tenets of the neurodiversity paradigm. I hope this explanation will help people to avoid this particular error in the future—and, when possible, to correct such misuse where they encounter it.

Examples of Correct Usage:

"We humans are a neurodiverse species."

"We employ a wide variety of creative teaching strategies to accommodate the many different learning styles represented in our highly neurodiverse student body."

"My neurodiverse family includes three neurotypicals, two autistics, and one person who's both ADHD and dyslexic."

"I think every single member of their board of directors is neurotypical. An organization that supposedly serves the needs of neurominority children should have a more neurodiverse board."

Examples of Incorrect Usage:

"This group welcomes autistics and other neurodiverse people." It's nice to be welcomed, but there's no such thing as a "neurodiverse person." the correct phrase here would be "autistics and other *neurodivergent* people."

"This group is open to both neurotypicals and the neurodiverse." No, no, no. "The neurodiverse?" Seriously? What does that even mean? The spectrum of neurodiversity encompasses the entire human species, so one can't label any subset of the human species as "the neurodiverse." And neurotypicals are part of the spectrum of human neurodiversity, so it makes no sense to say "neurotypicals and the neurodiverse," as if those were two separate things. The correct

way to say this would be, "This group is open to both neurotypicals and the *neurodivergent*."

I hope this list of definitions will help to foster greater clarity and understanding, and more accurate writing, when it comes to the terminology around neurodiversity. I encourage readers to share, cite, or quote from this piece, anywhere it might be useful. If you're writing up submission guidelines for neurodiversity-related writings, for a journal, anthology, conference, or other project, feel free to draw upon this piece in creating your guidelines. If you encounter a journalist who's doing a piece on a neurodiversity-related topic, or a group of college students who are writing about neurodiversity, please share this piece with them. And please feel free to use this piece as a resource in any situation in which there's confusion about what any of these terms mean.

Comments on "Neurodiversity: Some Basic Terms & Definitions"

These days the term *neurodiversity* is generally credited to Judy Singer, an Australian autistic sociologist who coined it in the late 1990s for a graduate thesis which was completed in 1998. However, I've met a couple of autistic elders who recall encountering and using the word even earlier in the 1990s, in the old email listserv discussions which were instrumental in the initial formation of autistic community. Perhaps it was just one of those ideas whose time had come, and it occurred to more than one autistic person around the same time.

I'm sure I'm not the only person who independently came up with *neurominority* and *the neurodiversity paradigm* in the first decade of the 21st century. Ralph Savarese and I came up with the term *neurocosmopolitanism* independently of one another (there'll be more about neurocosmopolitanism later on in the book), and Athena Lynn Michaels-Dillon and I originally came up with the term *neuroqueer* independently of one another as well (more about *that* later, too). Sometimes when the time is ripe for a concept to enter the world, it enters through multiple minds at once, the way modern calculus was developed independently and concurrently by Newton and Leibniz. In any event, even if Singer wasn't the very first to use it, I did get confirmation from her that the definition of *neurodiversity* I provide in "Neurodiversity: Some Basic Terms & Definitions" is consistent with her own understanding of the word.

•

As I mentioned near the end of the definition of *neurodivergent*, the terms *neurodivergent* and *neurodivergence* were coined in the year 2000 by Kassiane Asasumasu. Kassiane's a longtime friend who's been involved in the discourse on neurodiversity even longer than I have. When I first wrote this piece, I showed it to her and she gave her seal of approval to the way I'd explained her terms. So the definitions of those two terms in "Neurodiversity: Some Basic Terms & Definitions" are creator-authorized versions, as official as definitions get. (The same can be said for the definitions of the *neurodiversity paradigm* and *neurominority* provided in this piece, since I'm the one who coined those two terms in the first place.)

Neurodivergence is a value-neutral term that encompasses *any* significant divergence from dominant cultural norms of neurocognitive functioning—anything from autism to dyslexia to dyspraxia to aphantasia to synesthesia to epilepsy to schizophrenia to PTSD to Williams Syndrome to the cool stuff that long-term meditation practice does to the brains of Buddhist monks. Kassiane has repeatedly stated, in public and in private, that she intended the term to be as broadly inclusive as possible.

Unfortunately, as soon as the term started catching on, certain people started trying to redefine it more narrowly, in ways that directly violated Kassiane's inclusive intent. These people would often try to claim, for instance, that the term neurodivergence only referred to forms of neurodivergence that are innate genetic neurodevelopmental variants like autism.

It struck me that the main reason people were trying to distort the meaning of the word neurodivergence in this exclusionary way was because they were trying to talk about neurominority groups but they didn't have the word *neurominority*. So I coined the term *neurominority* in 2004 partly so that *I'd* have a term to use when I wanted to talk specifically about groups of people who all share similar forms of innate developmental neurodivergence for which they might encounter discrimination (e.g., autistic or dyslexic people), and partly so that *other* people would have a term for that purpose—and would thus, I hoped, stop misusing Kassiane's term.

Two decades later, I *still* encounter people who are trying to make the definitions of *neurodivergent* and *neurodivergence* narrower and less inclusive, or who have been taught an incorrect and exclusionary definition. As long as they're the sort of people who are open to learning (rather than the sort whose egos are so invested in being right that they aggressively double down on their errors), I sometimes find the problem can often be solved just by introducing them to the term *neurominority*, and explaining the distinction between *neurominority* and *neurodivergent*.

I'll say this one more time, because so many folks seem to have trouble grasping it: *neurodivergent* is not a euphemism for autistic, or for "autistic and/or ADHD," or anything along those lines. If you mean autistic, say autistic. If you mean "autistic and/or ADHD," say "autistic and/or ADHD." There are myriad possible ways to be neurodivergent, and many of them bear no resemblance whatsoever to autism or ADHD.

•

The single most common language error that people make, in writing or speaking about neurodiversity-related matters, is still the misuse of the word *neurodiverse* to mean *neurodivergent*. I already discuss this particular error at length in the "Terms & Definitions" piece itself. For the benefit anyone who's still confused about this particular issue, please allow me to boil it all down to three clear and simple rules:

1. Never, ever refer to yourself or any other individual as "neurodiverse." There is no such thing as a "neurodiverse person." The word you're looking for is *neurodivergent*.

2. Never, ever describe neurodivergent people or neurominority members collectively as "neurodiverse people."

3. Never, ever misuse "diverse" as a synonym or euphemism for "member of a marginalized or oppressed group," whether you're talking about neurodiversity, ethnic diversity, or any other form of diversity.

One thing I've learned about the error of misusing *neurodiverse* to mean *neurodivergent* is that it's an absolutely reliable indicator that the person making the error is a person whose thinking is still rooted in the pathology paradigm on some level, and who has simply misappropriated some neurodiversity-related terminology without actually bothering to study the neurodiversity paradigm or the work of the (mostly autistic) scholars and thinkers who developed the neurodiversity paradigm. It doesn't matter how well-known the person in question is, or what sort of credentials they boast; if they haven't learned words like *neurodivergent* and *neurominority*, and they're misusing the word *neurodiverse* instead, you can be 100%

sure that you're looking at a person who hasn't done their homework well enough to really know what they're talking about.

•

Finally, it's of the utmost importance to remember that the pathology paradigm and the neurodiversity paradigm are ways of understanding and relating to the phenomenon of human neurodiversity, and are foundations for practice—i.e., for how one treats one's fellow humans. The vocabulary that expresses the conceptual basis of a paradigm is an essential aspect of that paradigm, but the vocabulary itself is not the paradigm. Adopting the language of the neurodiversity paradigm isn't the same as actually making a meaningful shift in one's consciousness and one's practices.

I've found that the people who haven't truly made an internal shift to the neurodiversity paradigm, and are just appropriating the terminology of the neurodiversity paradigm while still operating based on the pathology paradigm, tend to use the terminology badly because they don't understand what it really means. But even if someone seems to be using the vocabulary of the neurodiversity paradigm well, that's no guarantee that they've made an authentic shift in their consciousness. If a person is talking about "overcoming neurodivergence," or is subjecting autistic children to "behavioral therapy" in order to make them act more like neurotypical children, they're still clearly operating based on the pathology paradigm regardless of what words they've adopted to disguise it.

•

The definitions I provide in "Neurodiversity: Some Basic Terms & Definitions," while still accurate, are simplified for the sake of brevity. Nowadays I feel that certain terms, like *neurodiversity* and *neurotypical*, require more nuanced explanation in order to adequately convey the complexity of the concepts and in order to discourage overly reductionist interpretations. I've attempted to convey these more nuanced understandings in the two chapters that follow this one.

Defining Neurodiversity

This brief essay is a new one, written especially for this book in the Summer of 2021. It started out as one of my comments on "Throw Away the Master's Tools," but it got long enough that I decided to give it its own chapter.

Neurodiversity is the variation among minds.

Each human being differs to some extent from every other human being, with respect to their neurocognitive functioning—how they think, perceive, know, and develop, how their minds process information and interact with the world. Neurodiversity is the name for this phenomenon.

Neurodiversity is an intrinsic characteristic of the human species. It is a diversity produced by a combination of multiple interacting factors, including the myriad possible permutations of genetics, the influence of developmental environments on genetic expression, and the infinite variety of ways in which each individual mind is shaped by culture, activity, environment, and experience throughout the lifespan.

In speaking of neurodiversity as the diversity among minds, I use the word *mind* in the broadest possible sense, to encompass the totality of every aspect of perception, cognition, emotion, memory, psyche, and consciousness.

Mind is an *embodied* phenomenon. The activity and development of the mind has a physical component in the form of electrochemical activity in the brain; the mind is encoded in the brain as ever-changing webs of neural connectivity. Changes in the brain create changes in the mind, and changes in the mind—new experiences, new mental activity—create changes in the brain. The brain, meanwhile, is not separate from the rest of the body; the body is a system of which the brain is one part, intricately interconnected with the rest by a vast network of nerves and blood vessels. The brain directs bodily activity and at the same time is continually affected and shaped by bodily activity and experience.

Mind is inextricably entwined with brain, and brain with body; thus, mind is inextricably entwined with body in a single complex system and in a continuous dance of mutual shaping. We're not minds riding around in vehicles of flesh and bone; we're *bodyminds*, bodies that think and perceive. Experience, awareness, sense of self, psychological development, and capacities for feeling, knowing, cognition, connection, and action are all entwined with—and shape, and are shaped by—habits of bodily usage, including habits of movement, posture, breath, contact, consumption, tension and relaxation, gaze, gesture, and expression.

If mind is an embodied phenomenon, it follows that the diversity of minds must also be a diversity of embodiments. Variations in neurocognitive functioning are entwined with variations in embodiment; autism, for example, involves distinctive modes of physicality and sensorimotor experience that are intimately connected with autistic modes of cognition. So when I say that neurodiversity is *the diversity among minds*, I'm really saying that it's *the diversity among bodyminds*.

It used to be commonplace for people to speak of neurodiversity as *diversity among brains*, and there are still people who speak about it that way. I think this is a mistake, an overly reductionist and essentialist definition that's decades behind present-day understandings of how human bodyminds work.

The persistence of this reductionist interpretation of neurodiversity is no doubt at least partly due to the fact that when most people see the prefix *neuro-*, they translate it as *brain*. But *neuro-* doesn't mean *brain*, it means *nerve*. In my view, the *neuro-* in *neurodiversity* is most usefully understood as referring not just to the brain but to the entire nervous system—and, by extension, to the full complexity of human cognition and the central role the nervous system plays in the embodied dance of consciousness.

Defining Neurotypicality & Neurodivergence

Like the previous essay, this is a new one written in the Summer of 2021—another piece that started out as a comment on "Throw Away the Master's Tools" and then grew into its own chapter.

The term *neurotypical* has been around since at least the early 1990s. It's a term that's widely misunderstood, and widely objected to by the people who misunderstand it. The standard objection goes something like this: "No one is neurotypical because everyone's brain is unique!" But in fact, the concept of neurotypicality is in no way incompatible with recognizing the uniqueness of every brain and every mind, and this argument against the term *neurotypical* is based in an inaccurate understanding of what the term means.

The false assumption underlying the "no one is neurotypical" argument is the assumption that *neurotypical* is just a synonym for *normal*. It's not. The neurodiversity paradigm rejects the whole idea that there's such a thing as a "normal brain" or a "normal mind." Belief in "normal" minds and brains is the hallmark of the pathology paradigm, so it would make no sense at all for the vocabulary of the neurodiversity paradigm to include a term that meant "having a normal mind or brain."

To understand what we *do* mean by neurotypical, let's draw an analogy between neurodiversity and the diversity of gender and sexuality. The pathology paradigm's construction and idealization of normativity pervades the dominant culture—which means that the majority of people in the world still behave *as if* there's such a thing as a normal brain or mind, in much the same way that the majority of people in the world still behave *as if* culturally constructed heteronormative gender roles are "normal" and "natural."

From earliest childhood, people are trained and pressured into the performance of *heteronormativity*—the performance of a restrictive binary heterosexual masculine or feminine gender role assigned to them at birth based on the shape of their genitalia. By the same token, people are trained and pressured from earliest childhood into the performance of *neuronormativity*—the performance of the local dominant culture's current prevailing images of how a so-called "normal" person with a so-called "normal" mind thinks and looks and behaves.

If you can perform your assigned heteronormative gender role convincingly enough throughout your life, *and* if staying within the boundaries of that performance is actually sustainable and bearable for you, *and* if you choose to stay within those boundaries and comply with the demands of heteronormativity, then the dominant culture judges your gender and sexuality to be "normal" and rewards you with cisgender privilege and straight privilege—in other words, the reward for your constant and convincing compliance with dominant standards of heteronormativity is that members and institutions of the dominant culture don't discriminate against you for being queer.

By the same token, if the functioning of your bodymind is such that it's possible and bearable for you convincingly maintain the performance of neuronormativity throughout your life, *and* if you choose to maintain that performance and comply with the dominant culture's standards of neuronormativity, then the dominant culture judges your mind to be "normal" and rewards you with neurotypical privilege—in other words, the reward for your constant and convincing compliance with dominant standards of neuronormativity is that members and institutions of the dominant culture don't discriminate against you for being "abnormal." This is what it means to be neurotypical.

So when we say someone is neurotypical, we don't mean they were born with a specific type of brain, and that the type of brain they were born with is the "normal" type—because that's just nonsense. There's no such thing as a normal brain or a normal "type of brain." In fact, while it can be useful to consider certain bodyminds in terms of categorizations like *autistic* or *dyslexic*, and while the bodyminds that fit into those categories often do appear to share certain distinguishing neurobiological characteristics, the whole idea of "types of brains" is ultimately rather dubious, or, at the very least, overly reductionist.

When we say someone is neurotypical, what we mean is that they live, act, and experience the world in a way that consistently falls within the boundaries of neuronormativity—i.e., within the boundaries of what the prevailing culture *imagines* a person with a "normal mind" to be like. That's quite different from saying that a person actually *has* a normal mind or a normal brain.

This queer-theory-informed understanding of the culturally constructed and situated nature of neurotypicality also enables us to better understand the meaning of the terms *neurodivergent* and *neurodivergence*. These terms, like the term *neurotypical*, are often objected to by well-intentioned people who don't fully understand their meanings. The usual objection is something along the lines of, "Calling a mind *divergent* implies that the mind diverges from normal, and I don't believe there's such a thing as a normal mind."

As already noted, though, the neurodiversity paradigm *also* rejects the idea that there's such a thing as a normal mind. When we call someone neurodivergent we don't mean that they aren't "normal," we mean that they aren't neurotypical.

In other words, what a neurodivergent person diverges from are the prevailing culturally constructed standards and culturally mandated performance of neuronormativity. Neurodivergence is divergence not from some "objective" state of normality (which, again, doesn't exist), but rather from whatever constructed image and performance of normality the prevailing culture currently seeks to impose.

Neurodivergence & Disability

Another chapter written especially for this book in 2021.

In many years of teaching college courses on autism and the neuro-diversity paradigm, not to mention incorporating material on autism and other forms of neurodivergence into various psychology courses, a troubling issue I've consistently encountered is that the vast majority of my students—even at the graduate level—arrive in my classroom entirely unfamiliar with the social model of disability. Since I'm planning to use this book as a textbook in at least one of my courses, I figure this is my chance to save myself from having to explain Disability Theory 101 all over again every semester. I can just write the explanation into the textbook, with particular focus on how it applies to the experience of autistic people and members of other pathologized neurominority groups.

The Medical Model vs the Social Model

There are two distinct models for understanding disability. One model is generally referred to, in the field of Disability Studies, as the *medical model of disability* (or sometimes, in the UK, the *individual model of disability*). The other model is generally referred to as the *social model of disability.* They're not the only possible models, but at present nearly all disability-related theory and praxis is based in one or the other of these two models.

In the medical model, the term *disability* refers to an impairment or defect which is seen as being located in the body and/or mind of an individual. Through the lens of the medical model, in other words, a person is seen as "having" a disability. The medical model is currently the prevailing model in the modern world, and has been for quite some time, which means it's the understanding of disability that most people have picked up by default unless they've actively looked for an alternative and/or done some serious critical thinking on the subject. The medical model is highly compatible with capitalism and other related aspects of the prevailing culture. When it comes to the discourse on autism and various other marginalized neurocognitive styles, the medical model is deeply entwined with the pathology paradigm.

The social model of disability emerged within the disability rights movement and remains a cornerstone of disability rights activism, as well as being a foundational concept in the field of Disability Studies. When it comes to the discourse on autism and various other marginalized neurocognitive styles, the social model is deeply entwined with the neurodiversity paradigm and the neurodiversity movement. In the social model, *disabled* is understood as the opposite of *enabled*. Society is set up to meet the needs of people with a specific set of traits, needs, and abilities. Those privileged people are *abled*, or *enabled*—in other words, society is set up to enable their participation.

Within the social model of disability, when we say that a person is disabled, we mean that society isn't properly set up to enable their participation, and instead is often set up in a way that creates barriers to their participation (e.g., building staircases without ramps or good working elevators is a barrier to wheelchair users; the expectation of eye contact in job interviews is a barrier to autistic people). Thus, those people whose needs differ significantly from those of the dominant majority are *disabled* by society rather than *enabled*.

Where the medical model is reductionist, the social model is far more complex and nuanced because disability is understood as always being contingent upon the context in which the individual is currently operating. In other words, disability is not a static condition located within the individual (as per the medical model) but instead is a phenomenon that manifests in varying ways and varying degrees depending upon the nature and degree of the mismatch between the individual's needs and the way those needs are accommodated in the context of a given situation or societal surround.

Unlike the medical model, the social model makes a crucial distinction between *disability* and *impairment*. An impairment is when an individual lacks some specific capacity that the majority of individuals possess. In the medical model disability and impairment are viewed as effectively synonymous. In the social model, however, an impairment creates an atypical set of access needs, and disability is what happens when those needs aren't sufficiently accommodated. You're *dis*abled to whatever degree your participation isn't properly *en*abled within a given setting.

Understood through the lens of the social model, then, disability (or disablement) is a form of marginalization. This is why the phrase *person with a disability* is part of the language of the medical model: it's a phrase that implies that the disability is located entirely within the bodymind of the person, rather than in the way the external environment fails to meet the person's access needs.

In the social model, people don't have disabilities; people are disabled. In the social model, a phrase like *person with a disability* is nonsensical; it's like saying *person with a marginalization* or *person with an oppression*. And that disgusting ableist euphemism *differently abled* is even more ridiculous; it's like describing members of an oppressed group as *differently privileged*.

A Few Examples

Let's start with a relatively simple example to help make the social model of disability more clear: if you can't walk, that's what's known as a mobility impairment. Are you disabled? Yes, but here's the crucial piece that the social model highlights: the precise degree to which you're disabled depends on how well your access needs are accommodated.

If you can't walk, a wheelchair is an invaluable accommodation. If you live in a society that hasn't invented wheelchairs or only has the clunkiest of old-fashioned wheelchairs, you're going to be more disabled than if you live in a society that provides all its mobility-impaired citizens with high-quality electric wheelchairs. If you live in a town where most of the buildings (and public transit stations and other structures) have stairs but no ramps or elevators, and where most of the doorways are absurdly narrow, then you're going to be much more disabled than you would be if you lived in a town in which all of the structures are built with wheelchair access in mind.

Note also that social *attitudes* are a key component in the dynamics of enablement and disablement: an office building might have state-of-the-art ramps and elevators and wide automatic doors, but none of that will matter much if the people who work in the building are unwilling to hire a wheelchair user.

Moving on to an example that's specifically neurodivergence-related: in the dyslexic bodymind, the impairment is in the capacity to process visual detail in a linear two-dimensional fashion, which of course affects the ability to read and spell. This impairment seems to be just an inconvenient side effect of a neurocognitive processing style that also comes with significant strengths in areas like 3-D spatial processing and nonlinear big-picture thinking. And here's where it gets interesting, from a social model of disability perspective: it's a side effect that only becomes a significant inconvenience in cultures and contexts in which it's important to be able to read.

Dyslexia, like autism and various other forms of innate neurodivergence, has likely existed within the human species for a very long time, probably since our prehistoric hunter-gatherer days. For most of that vast span of time, societal participation and the meeting of societal demands haven't required the ability to quickly and accurately process a lot of linear strings of written or typed letters and words on flat surfaces—which means that for most of the time dyslexia has been around, being dyslexic hasn't meant being disabled at all. And within the next few centuries, it's possible that dyslexic people will go back to not being disabled at all, either because massive societal collapse makes literacy less relevant, or because massive technological advancement brings us to a stage where the reading and writing of linear text is largely supplanted by engagement with information in multisensory 3-D virtual interfaces. Dyslexia thus serves as a particularly clear illustration of the context-dependent nature of disability.

And with dyslexia, again, attitudes are part of the social context that enables or disables. A dyslexic child is far more disabled by a school environment in which they're shamed and written off as "stupid" for their reading difficulties, than by a school environment that responds to those same difficulties by immediately providing accommodations, taking a strengths-based approach to the child's development, teaching the child what dyslexia is in a non-stigmatizing way, and providing the child with examples of positive dyslexic role models. When proponents of the reductionist medical model describe a dyslexic child as "having a learning disability," they promote ableism by framing the disability as a defect located within the child (i.e., as something the child "has"), and by thus directing attention away from the child's environment and the ways in which the local education system might be functioning to disable the child rather than enable them.

Finally, let's consider the example of a hypothetical autistic individual who has no significant difficulty with motor coordination, can readily handle any sensory experiences they're likely to encounter in day-to-day life in the modern world, and is cognitively capable of executing all the tasks that are assigned in whatever school or professional environment they find themselves in. Now let's also say that this autistic person's physical mannerisms are quite visibly autistic: rocking back and forth; no eye contact or imitation of neurotypical expressions; distinctively autistic hand and head motions (you'll know what I'm talking about if you've hung out with enough autistic folks who haven't been forced to suppress their natural embodiment styles). And add to this a distinctively autistic communication style (statements, questions, and answers that are direct, blunt, truthful, and literal).

In the context of the prevailing social milieu, this person is going to be disabled, because their autistic style of embodiment and communication will result in social rejection, discrimination, misunderstanding, disrespect, exclusion, and abuse by the majority of non-autistic people they encounter. A multitude of doors will be closed to them; they'll have undue difficulty getting or keeping jobs (or other useful things, like apartments); their performance at school and work will be seriously impacted by the hostility of peers and authority figures; they'll have a hard time getting any assistance they need from others (including those whose jobs are supposed to involve protecting people from abuse and discrimination). All this adds up to some pretty significant disablement.

What makes this particular example such an interesting study in the social model of disability and the dynamics of disablement is that this person's styles of embodiment and communication aren't actual functional *impairments* in any objective sense. The autistic person in this example is disabled *entirely* as a result of societal attitudes—specifically, the prevailing culture's intolerance for divergence from the dominant norms of neurotypical social performance. The accommodations this person needs in order to enable their full societal access and participation consist entirely of changes to social attitudes.

(Note that a great many autistic people do also have specific impairments that require more material accommodation—for instance, non-speaking autistics who need access to assistive communication technologies, or autistics with the sort of sensory sensitivities that are best accommodated through adjustments to physical environments. But autistics like the one in the preceding example, who don't have such impairments and whose disablement could be alleviated entirely through shifts in social attitudes without any substantial material or logistical accommodation, also exist, and I've chosen to focus the preceding example on such a person for purposes of more clearly illustrating one particular aspect of the social dynamics of disablement.)

Autism & Disability

In the interest of clearing up a common misconception, I want to address a couple of specific points regarding the disablement of autistic people. Some people, working from incomplete and inaccurate understandings of the neurodiversity paradigm, somehow arrive at the false impression that the neurodiversity paradigm implies that autistic people aren't disabled. This is a gross misinterpretation.

Recall that the fundamental principles of the neurodiversity paradigm are that neurodiversity is one form of human diversity; that there's no one "right" or "normal" type of mind; and that the social dynamics that manifest in regard to neurodiversity are similar to the social dynamics that manifest in regard to other forms of human diversity. None of these principles in any way contradicts or precludes the idea that some neurodivergent people might be disabled.

And in fact, modern society—a society which by and large is designed exclusively around neurotypical needs and expectations, and is unrelentingly hostile to deviation from neurotypical norms—systematically disables a great many neurodivergent people, autistic people included. Within the present social milieu, autistic people are almost always disabled to at least some degree.

The reason that so many autistic rights activists and other folks interested in fostering autistic well-being have embraced the neurodiversity paradigm, and are opposed to framing autism as a pathology (e.g., a "disorder" or "condition"), isn't that we're pretending autistic people aren't disabled. Rather, it's that we've observed that the pathology paradigm serves to exacerbate rather than mitigate autistic disablement.

The assumption that autism is intrinsically pathological, intrinsically a problem or form of wrongness, leads inevitably to the assumption that the well-being of any given autistic person hinges on that autistic person somehow becoming less autistic. This in turn has the effect of keeping discourse and praxis focused on eliminating or "treating" autism—using methods that are consistently harmful to autistic people, such as abusive behaviorist approaches or pseudo-biomedical quackery—at the expense of any substantial focus on actions that would actually improve autistic people's quality of life.

The framework of the neurodiversity paradigm, on the other hand, supports approaches based in the social model of disability. If we start by recognizing autistic people as a marginalized group, we can see that their disablement is part of their marginalization; i.e., part of how autistics are marginalized within the present social milieu is that their access needs aren't properly accommodated. We can also see that the pathology paradigm itself is one of the factors that contributes to autistic disablement—for instance, framing autism as a pathology fosters a societal mindset in which autistic modes of embodiment, expression, and communication are stigmatized as pathological symptoms rather than accommodated.

The neurodiversity paradigm, properly understood and applied in conjunction with the social model of disability, thus suggests an approach to autistic well-being based in de-pathologizing autism, accepting autistic people as autistic people, and actively working to enable the full societal inclusion of autistic people by finding better ways to accommodate their access needs. Enablement as the solution to disablement.

This is why if you ask me whether autism is a disability, I'll say no, but if you ask me whether autistic people are disabled, I'll say yes. To people who don't understand the distinction between the medical model of disability and the social model of disability, "autism is a disability" and "autistic people are disabled" might seem like they mean the same thing. But the implications of these two phrases are actually quite different. "Autism is a disability" essentially means "autism is a pathology or deficit," whereas "autistic people are disabled" essentially means "autistic people's needs are not properly accommodated by the world around them in a way that enables their societal participation."

To say "autism is a disability" is to perpetuate the frameworks of the pathology paradigm and the medical model of disability, by framing autism as a problem located within the autistic individual. To say "autistic people are disabled," by contrast, embraces the frameworks of the neurodiversity paradigm and the social model of disability—and opens the door to better approaches to autistic well-being—by framing autistic disablement as being the result of correctible mismatches between autistic needs and societal accommodations.

Not All Neurodivergent People Are Disabled

In wrapping up this discussion of neurodivergence and disability, I want clarify one final point: *not all neurodivergent people are disabled*.

Neurodivergence is a broadly inclusive term that means *any significant divergence from dominant cultural norms of neurocognitive functioning*. Kassiane Asasumasu, who coined the terms *neurodivergence* and *neurodivergent* way back in the year 2000, has consistently emphasized that she intended the terms to be interpreted as inclusively as possible—i.e., that when she says *any* significant divergence from dominant cultural norms of neurocognitive functioning, she means *any* significant divergence. In all the time I've known her and followed her writings, Kassiane has never once said, "Oh, wait, I only mean the forms of divergence that are pathologized," or "Oh, wait, when I said that neurodivergent people are people whose neurocognitive functioning diverges from dominant norms, I only meant the disabled ones."

Any significant divergence. That includes both innate forms of divergence (e.g., autism, dyslexia, aphantasia, Down Syndrome) and forms of divergence that can be acquired during the lifespan (e.g., the lasting neurocognitive effects of various sorts of trauma and/or extensive drug use).

There are innate forms of neurodivergence that don't involve any sort of disablement. Many forms of synesthesia, for example. While it's possible to have levels of synesthesia so intense as to result in atypical access needs which require accommodation, the majority of people who experience synesthesia aren't impaired by it in any significant way, and thus require no special accommodation for it, and thus aren't disabled by the absence of such accommodation.

As for *acquired* forms of neurodivergence that don't involve disablement, the wonders of human neuroplasticity make it possible for people to alter their neurocognitive functioning in all sorts of interesting ways, some of which are both long-lasting and clearly divergent from dominant norms. I know a number of people who've permanently altered their neurocognitive functioning through the use of psychedelic drugs, without becoming disabled (i.e., they're still able to fully access, participate in, and thrive within the systems, structures, and institutions of the dominant culture).

A few of the old friends I used to take LSD with, for instance, have reported that some of the visual effects of that marvelous drug never entirely went away for them; decades later, they still see trails and auras, and still find that every blank wall they look at morphs into a writhing tapestry of color. This hasn't impaired them in any way or necessitated any accommodations, but it's obviously not "normal" by the standards of conventional society. (I can't say for sure whether my own youthful LSD use had any such lasting sensory effect, because trails and auras and writhing surfaces and other such visual embellishments have been part of my autistic sensory reality since I was born.)

Another example would be the neurocognitive effects of long-term meditation practice. Neuroimaging studies on Buddhist monks have demonstrated that extensive engagement in meditation practices over a long period of time results not only in lasting alterations to consciousness and neurocognitive functioning, but also in significant and measurable changes to the thickness of the prefrontal cortex. So experienced Buddhist monks and other lifelong meditation practitioners come to diverge from neurotypical norms on a neurobiological level and certainly on a cognitive level (anyone who's spent time with a zen master can tell you that they think very differently from just about anyone else). And yet, meditation clearly doesn't lead to disablement; in fact, many long-term meditation practitioners, myself included, have found that meditation-induced neurodivergences can actually be quite helpful in navigating modern life and can even help to mitigate the challenges posed by some other forms of neurodivergence.

So please recognize that a great many neurodivergent people are disabled. Please learn to see how societal prejudices and failures of accommodation serve to create this disablement, and please look for ways in which you can help to challenge these prejudices and remedy these failures of accommodation. But also, please respect the inclusive intentions of the person who gave us the word *neurodivergence*; please don't attempt to redefine the word in ways that exclude non-disabled neurodivergent people.

Reflections on Neurocosmopolitanism

And let's wrap up Part I of this book with one more new piece written in 2021...

I've been involved in the neurodiversity movement since it was just a ragtag scattering of scrappy autistic activists connecting with one another on early internet platforms, and I've been involved in laying the foundations of the field of Neurodiversity Studies since long before anyone was calling it a field. Through it all, a central aim of my work has been to help bring about a paradigm shift in how the prevailing culture understands and engages with human neurodiversity—a shift away from the currently-dominant pathology paradigm, toward what I've long referred to as the neurodiversity paradigm.

To create a better future, one must first be able to *imagine* a better future. Working to eliminate specific problems is often necessary but ultimately insufficient; it's essential to also have some positive guiding vision of what one is working *toward*. When working to bring about transformation on any scale from the personal to the global, it's vital to ask oneself what it might look like if one's work were to someday succeed in the fullest possible way. Those of us engaged in the work of fostering a cultural shift from the pathology paradigm to the neurodiversity paradigm would thus do well to reflect upon two questions:

1. What sort of attitude or approach toward neurodiversity might one find in individuals who have truly comprehended, embraced, and integrated the neurodiversity paradigm?

2. What sort of attitude or approach toward neurodiversity might one find in a society that has fully embraced and been transformed by the neurodiversity paradigm?

My own answer, in both cases, is encapsulated in the term *neurocosmopolitanism* (a term coined by my fellow neurodiversity scholar Ralph Savarese and myself, independently of one another and more or less concurrently). An individual who has truly comprehended, embraced, and integrated the neurodiversity paradigm is likely to exhibit neurocosmopolitan attitudes, and a society that has fully embraced and been transformed by the neurodiversity paradigm would be a neurocosmopolitan society. So, what does that mean? What *is* neurocosmopolitanism?

Cosmopolitanism is the open-minded embracing of human diversity. The term is traditionally used in regard to the diversity of cultures, ethnicities, and nationalities; *cosmopolite* literally translates as *citizen of the world*. The cosmopolite regards all humanity as ultimately part of a single global community—an essential unity which is in no way invalidated by the differences among us, and which in fact has the potential to be greatly enriched by those differences when we engage with them in a spirit of humility, respect, and openness to learning.

Neurocosmopolitanism consists of approaching neurodiversity in the same spirit in which the cosmopolite approaches cultural diversity. To embrace the neurodiversity paradigm is to refuse to pathologize neurocognitive styles and experiences that differ from our own, and to accept neurodiversity as a natural, healthy, and important form of human biodiversity—a fundamental and vital characteristic of the human species, a crucial source of evolutionary and creative potential. Neurocosmopolitanism goes beyond this baseline of acceptance, though, just as cosmopolitanism goes beyond mere tolerance of cultural differences. The neurocosmopolitan seeks to actively engage with and preserve human neurodiversity, and to honor, explore, and cultivate its creative potentials, in a spirit of humility, respect, and continual openness to learning and transformation.

Cosmopolitanism's opposite is provincialism. In the context of the diversity of cultures and nationalities, provincialism boils down to viewing one's own native culture and people as the default "normal" culture and people, and other cultures and peoples as exotic, inferior, threatening, inhuman, and/or just plain "wrong" to whatever extent they differ from one's own. One might say, then, that the pathology paradigm, with its privileging of particular bodyminds and particular modes of cognition and behavior as "normal" and implicitly superior, is a form of *neuroprovincialism*.

A neurocosmopolitan perspective, by contrast, privileges no bodymind as the "natural" default way of being, nor as more "normal" or intrinsically correct than any other, just as a hallmark of cosmopolitanism is the recognition that no one culture is more intrinsically correct, natural, or "normal" than any other. The neurocosmopolite welcomes and appreciates the differences among bodyminds—all the manifold variations in perception, cognition, embodiment, experience, needs, and styles of communication and interaction—in the same open-minded and profoundly egalitarian spirit with which the true cosmopolite greets cultural differences.

The development of a truly cosmopolitan spirit necessarily involves transcending racism, nationalism, and delusions of cultural supremacy. A racist cosmopolite would be a contradiction in terms, at least by any definition of cosmopolitanism I'd consider worthy of the name. And yet, while transcendence of these various ugly manifestations of provincialism is obviously a fundamental prerequisite for cosmopolitanism, their mere absence does not in itself constitute cosmopolitanism. There are various understandings of cosmopolitanism, but the versions of cosmopolitan thought toward which I lean go far beyond mere tolerance and acceptance of human diversity. In the forms of cosmopolitanism that serve as models for how I envision neurocosmopolitanism, the cosmopolite actively welcomes, celebrates, and engages with the differences among us as sources of learning, growth, and mutual aesthetic, intellectual, cultural, and creative enrichment.

The same can be said in regard to neurocosmopolitanism. The cultivation of a neurocosmopolitan attitude necessarily involves unlearning and transcending the neuroprovincialist mindset of the pathology paradigm—in other words, making the shift to the neurodiversity paradigm. This paradigm shift is as much an essential prerequisite for the emergence of neurocosmopolitanism as the unlearning of racism, nationalism, and cultural chauvinism are prerequisites for cosmopolitanism. To view the bodyminds of neurominority members through the lens of pathology—e.g., to frame autism and other minority modes of neurocognitive functioning as "conditions," or to rank the functioning of human bodyminds as "high" or "low" based on the degree to which they conform to some particular set of cultural norms of performance—is fundamentally incompatible with the neurocosmopolitan spirit in the same way that the framing of certain ethnic groups as "superior" or "inferior" is incompatible with cosmopolitanism.

At the same time, the neurodiversity paradigm is by no means synonymous with neurocosmopolitanism. The shift from the pathology paradigm to the neurodiversity paradigm doesn't lead inevitably to the emergence of full-blown neurocosmopolitanism, it's just an essential first step. True neurocosmopolitanism goes further, as Ralph Savarese implied when he gave one of his essays on neurocosmopolitanism the subtitle "Beyond Mere Acceptance and Inclusion." True neurocosmopolitanism, like true cosmopolitanism, extends beyond the mere acceptance and accommodation of the differences among us, to an active embracing of and engagement with those differences as potential sources of growth, enrichment, and creative synergy.

The mere presence of neurodivergent individuals cannot serve on its own to augment the creative power of a group or organization or society, if having a real voice within that group or society is contingent upon acting neurotypical and upon only making the sort of social contributions that don't trouble the collective trance of neuronormativity. The true creative potentials of neurodiversity can be realized, within any given environment, only to the extent that people are empowered to participate in the ongoing collective co-creation and shaping of that environment while openly acting in ways that violate the constraints of neuronormative performance.

Although we live in a world in which the prevailing attitudes toward cultural, ethnic, and national differences are often far from cosmopolitan, individual cosmopolites nonetheless abound. By the same token, any individual who's learned to see beyond the narrow distorting lens of the pathology paradigm can cultivate a neurocosmopolitan approach to life.

My hope is that some readers will be inspired not only to begin generating their own visions of a neurocosmopolitan future, but also to share and discuss those emerging visions in a variety of contexts—and thus to inspire others toward their own neurocosmopolitan futurist imaginings and toward participation in further dialogues about those imaginings, so that collective and collaborative visions of possible neurocosmopolitan futures can eventually emerge to provide a greater sense of direction for the work of the neurodiversity movement and the field of Neurodiversity Studies.

I've found the thought experiment of imagining a neurocosmopolitan future to be both consistently productive and inspiring, and consistently challenging. Challenging, because the pathology paradigm is so deeply and pervasively ingrained in present-day society that it currently shapes even the neurodiversity movement itself, along with most neurodiversity scholarship. Having emerged in opposition to the abuse, stigmatization, and marginalization of neurominorities that are the inevitable consequences of the pathology paradigm, the neurodiversity movement—and much of the existing neurodiversity scholarship so far—has been largely defined by that quite necessary opposition. Part of the challenge of imagining a truly neurocosmopolitan future is that it means imagining not merely a future in which the neurodiversity movement has made substantial progress in its goals, but a future in which those goals may have been so well achieved as to render the movement obsolete.

I offer the following questions to spark reflection and imagination. This short list of questions is obviously far from comprehensive; I mean them as "sample questions," intended not only to inspire thoughts about possible neurocosmopolitan futures but also to inspire the formulation of further questions along similar lines:

What might education look like in a system in which the acceptance, inclusion, and accommodation of every sort of bodymind represents an unquestioned baseline? What if "acceptance and inclusion" didn't mean neurodivergent students being accepted and included under neurotypical supervision within educational environments created by and for neurotypicals, but instead meant a system which has itself been shaped through the collaboration of a wide diversity of minds—a system sufficiently neurocosmopolitan as to place all students on equal footing and render the concepts of "typical" and "divergent" effectively irrelevant? What might classroom education look like at various levels from preschool through grad school, in the context of a neurocosmopolitan approach to education in which it's built into the curriculum that every person in the class, teachers and students alike, works at learning to comprehend and accommodate the neurocognitive styles and communication needs of every other person in the class as best they can? What if both the education of youth and adults, and the training of educators, included the explicit understanding that no neurocognitive style is more "correct" or "normal" than any other, and that the work of mutual accommodation is both an essential part of a proper education and an essential preparation for being a participating citizen in a civilized society?

What might the results be if it were standard practice for organizations to actively seek to cultivate neurodiversity within their ranks at every level, including the highest levels of leadership and policy-making? What might organizations and social institutions look like, if conformity to some particular set of neurocognitive norms was not in any way—officially or unofficially—an advantage in attaining entry, employment, inclusion, advancement, or positions of leadership? What if cultivation of neurodiversity within organizational ranks didn't consist merely of neurodivergent individuals being brought into neurotypical-run organizational environments under neurotypical supervision, but instead occurred in the context of neurocosmopolitan organizational environments in which the systems, structures, and policies were created collaboratively under the leadership of a wide diversity of minds—with no one sort of mind privileged over others or considered the default norm?

Cosmopolitanism has historically functioned as a source of cultural enrichment and creative innovation by creating opportunities for the process of mutual adaptation and transformative fusion known as *hybridization*. When cross-cultural interactions are navigated within a cosmopolitan spirit, rather than with provincial prejudices or colonialist agendas of domination, it fosters mutually beneficial cultural exchanges and the creative hybridizations and synergies which have in myriad ways shaped music, art, language, literature, spirituality, philosophy, aesthetics, science, and technology throughout history and into the present day. How much more of what the philosopher Edgar Morin calls "the genius of diversity" might be awakened in a society that was not only truly cosmopolitan in its engagement with cultural diversity, but also truly neurocosmopolitan in its engagement with neurodiversity? What new confluences, creative hybridizations, and transformative synergies might emerge, on every scale in every realm of society and culture, and what might the results look like?

We're a long ways from a neurocosmopolitan society, but it's a goal worth working toward and a vision that serves to guide and inspire much of my work. Perhaps it will guide and inspire you as well. And while we work toward this perhaps distant goal, each one of us can cultivate the neurocosmopolitan spirit in our own minds and in our own lives, right here and right now.

PART II:
AUTISTIC EMPOWERMENT

"Our essential task in life is to awaken to the way that the eternal would speak through us, to learn to live out our intended personality and the inner weirdness that makes us a unique torchbearer of the flame of life."

Michael Meade

The Story Behind
"What Is Autism?"

From 2012 to 2018, I worked with the Multidisciplinary Association for Psychedelic Studies (MAPS) as a consultant on a groundbreaking research study which we eventually published in the journal *Psychopharmacology* (vol. 235, no. 11, June 2018) under the accurate but cumbersome title "Reduction in Social Anxiety After MDMA-Assisted Psychotherapy with Autistic Adults: A Randomized, Double-Blind, Placebo-Controlled Pilot Study."

This was the first formal psychopharmacological study of autistic subjects to be grounded in the neurodiversity paradigm rather than the pathology paradigm. There was nothing in the study that pathologized autistic people for being autistic, or that framed autism as inferior to neurotypicality. It wasn't in any way about "treating autism" (a concept as innately oppressive as the concept of "treating homosexuality"). It was about treating social anxiety in consenting adult autistics who wanted to stop experiencing social anxiety.

We did the whole study and subsequent journal article without using the language of the pathology paradigm. Where researchers mired in the pathology paradigm might have framed social anxiety as a "symptom" of autism or a "comorbid condition" (thus implicitly framing autism as a pathological "condition"), we explicitly acknowledged that social anxiety in the autistic population was a symptom of the extensive social trauma neurotypical society inflicts upon autistics from childhood—in other words, that what we sought to treat was a symptom not of autism but of traumatic oppression.

My friend and colleague Alicia Danforth, one of the lead researchers on the study, did a brief interview with me about it via email for the Spring 2014 issue of the *MAPS Bulletin*. The study was still in the proposal stage at that time, and the MAPS audience on the whole wasn't any more knowledgeable about autism than the rest of the general public, so the idea behind the interview was to help this audience understand the important distinction between "treating autism" (ugh) and treating a trauma-related anxiety issue for which a significant number of autistic folks wanted an effective treatment.

Alicia's first question to me in the interview was "What is your definition of autism?" When I'd typed out my response, I realized I'd created something which up until that point hadn't existed and was badly needed: a clear, concise, accessible explanation of autism which was based in the neurodiversity paradigm rather than the pathology paradigm. In March of 2014, weeks before that interview appeared in the *MAPS Bulletin*, I published my explanation of autism on my website under the title "What Is Autism?" I included this introduction:

> *How many websites are there that have a page called something like "What Is Autism?" or "About Autism"? How often do organizations, professionals, scholars, and others need to include a few paragraphs of basic introductory "What Is Autism?" text in a website, brochure, presentation, or academic paper?*

I've seen so many versions of that obligatory "What Is Autism" or "About Autism" text. And they're almost all terrible. For starters, almost all of them—even the versions written by people who claim to be in favor of "autism acceptance" or to support the neurodiversity paradigm—use the language of the pathology paradigm, which intrinsically contributes to the oppression of autistics.

On top of that, most of these descriptions of autism – even many of the descriptions written by autistics – propagate inaccurate information and false stereotypes. Some are so bad that they actually quote the DSM.

Of course, there are also a few really good pieces of "What Is Autism" text out there. But for the most part, they're rather personal pieces, about the authors' own unique experiences of autism, rather than general introductory definitions. What is needed is some good basic introductory "What Is Autism" text that is:

1.   consistent with current evidence;

2.   not based in the pathology paradigm;

3.   concise, simple, and accessible;

4.   formal enough for professional and academic use.

Since I couldn't find such a piece of text elsewhere, I wrote one. And here it is. I hereby give everyone permission to reprint the text below, in whole or in part, whenever you need a piece of basic "What Is Autism" or "About Autism" text. Please do credit me for writing it. But really, as long as credit is given, anyone can go ahead and use this text for free.

A lot of folks have taken me up on that invitation. Where "Neurodiversity: Some Basic Terms & Definitions" is the piece of my writing that's been most widely cited in other people's writing so far, "What Is Autism?" is the piece that's been most widely reprinted, quoted, adapted, and translated. As of this writing in 2021, there are translations of "What Is Autism?" available online in Spanish, Portuguese, Russian, German, Swedish, Czech, Slovene, and Estonian.

The MAPS study was a great success, by the way. Our study participants did indeed show statistically significant long-term reductions in social anxiety symptoms in the wake of their MDMA-assisted psychotherapy sessions. We also showed that it was possible to get federal approval for a research study with autistic participants (one currently needs approval from both the FDA and the DEA to use a controlled substance like MDMA in a research study), and possible to subsequently get the results of that study published in a prestigious scientific journal, without once disrespecting the autistic participants by using the language of the pathology paradigm.

What Is Autism?

Autism is a genetically-based human neurological variant. The complex set of interrelated characteristics that distinguish autistic neurology from non-autistic neurology is not yet fully understood, but current evidence indicates that the central distinction is that autistic brains are characterized by particularly high levels of synaptic connectivity and responsiveness. This tends to make the autistic individual's subjective experience more intense and chaotic than that of non-autistic individuals: on both the sensorimotor and cognitive levels, the autistic mind tends to register more information, and the impact of each bit of information tends to be both stronger and less predictable.

Autism is a developmental phenomenon, meaning that it begins *in utero* and has a pervasive influence on development, on multiple levels, throughout the lifespan. Autism produces distinctive, atypical ways of thinking, moving, interaction, and sensory and cognitive processing. One analogy that has often been made is that autistic individuals have a different neurological "operating system" than non-autistic individuals.

According to current estimates, somewhere between one percent and two percent of the world's population is autistic. While the number of individuals diagnosed as autistic has increased continually over the past few decades, evidence suggests that this increase in diagnosis is the result of increased public and professional awareness, rather than an actual increase in the prevalence of autism.

Despite underlying neurological commonalities, autistic individuals are vastly different from one another. Some autistic individuals exhibit exceptional cognitive talents. However, in the context of a society designed around the sensory, cognitive, developmental, and social needs of non-autistic individuals, autistic individuals are almost always disabled to some degree—sometimes quite obviously, and sometimes more subtly.

The realm of social interaction is one context in which autistic individuals tend to consistently be disabled. An autistic child's sensory experience of the world is more intense and chaotic than that of a non-autistic child, and the ongoing task of navigating and integrating that experience thus occupies more of the autistic child's attention and energy. This means the autistic child has less attention and energy available to focus on the subtleties of social interaction. Difficulty meeting the social expectations of non-autistics often results in social rejection, which further compounds social difficulties and impedes social development. For this reason, autism has been frequently misconstrued as being essentially a set of "social and communication deficits," by those who are unaware that the social challenges faced by autistic individuals are just by-products of the intense and chaotic nature of autistic sensory and cognitive experience.

Autism is still widely regarded as a "disorder," but this view has been challenged in recent years by proponents of the neurodiversity model, which holds that autism and other neurocognitive variants are simply part of the natural spectrum of human biodiversity, like variations in ethnicity or sexual orientation (which have also been pathologized in the past). Ultimately, to describe autism as a disorder represents a value judgment rather than a scientific fact.

Autism and Social Trauma

As previously noted, my "What Is Autism?" piece was originally written as an answer to a question in Alicia Danforth's interview with me for the MAPS Bulletin in 2014. Later on in that same interview, in answer to a question about the rationale behind studying ways to treat social anxiety in the autistic population, I shared a few thoughts that I figure might be worth sharing again here...

Many autistics suffer from some degree of social anxiety—a fear and anxiety response around social interaction. The crucial thing to understand is that social anxiety is not intrinsic to autism. Intense and atypical sensory experiences, and atypical styles of physical movement, are innate to autistic neurocognitive processing; if one is autistic, such experiences are going to be part of one's reality to some degree. But that's not necessarily the case with social anxiety.

To non-autistics, autistic people almost always come across as socially "odd" in some way—sometimes very much so. Indeed, as already noted, it's become a widespread error in the field of psychology to misconstrue autism as being primarily a set of "social and communication deficits."

A more accurate and less biased way of looking at it is that the communication difficulties between autistics and non-autistics run both ways: autistics have trouble understanding and communicating with non-autistics, and non-autistics have trouble understanding and communicating with autistics. This makes perfect sense: of course it's challenging to understand someone whose mind works very differently from one's own.

But because autistics are very much in the minority and hold less power in society, communication difficulties between an autistic and a non-autistic are always attributed to a deficit on the part of an autistic person. One rarely hears it pointed out that a non-autistic person suffers from an impaired ability to understand autistics. As the political scientist Karl Deutsch once noted, power is "the ability not to have to learn."

The upshot of all this is that the vast majority of autistic people experience frequent social rejection and hostility, beginning in very early childhood. Most autistics today constantly receive the message—again, starting in very early childhood—that the ways they naturally think, feel, move, and communicate are all wrong; that who they are is wrong.

This constant social rejection is deeply painful and traumatic. When such experiences are the norm in a person's vulnerable formative years, of course that person is going to come to see social interaction as a venture into a minefield, a miserable and frightening experience likely to erupt without warning into yet another experience of pain, failure, and humiliation. Unfortunately, this often becomes a self-fulfilling prophecy, since no one is at their best socially when they're experiencing overwhelming fear and anxiety. So the early history of social rejection causes social anxiety, which impairs social performance, resulting in further negative social experiences that reinforce the trauma.

Therein lies the key point, and the cause for hope and optimism: the social anxiety that afflicts so many autistics isn't inherent to autism—it is, instead, a symptom of trauma. And trauma can be healed.

Person-First Language Is the Language of Autistiphobic Bigots

This piece is a new one, written in 2021. A number of autistic authors have written critiques of person-first language in the past, beginning with Jim Sinclair's "Why I Dislike Person First Language" in 1999. While these previous critiques have articulated excellent points with which I'm largely in agreement, I haven't been entirely satisfied with them; I've yet to encounter one that offers sufficient critical analysis of the purposes and rationales behind person-first language. So I wrote my own, and here it is.

If you have even the slightest familiarity with the societal discourse on autism—whether you've learned about autism in an academic or professional setting, or just been exposed to discussions about it in the mass media—you've almost certainly encountered person-first language. That's where instead of simply referring to autistic people as autistic people, folks use grotesque and needlessly cumbersome phrases like *people with autism, children who have autism, individuals experiencing autism,* or *adults living with autism.*

Person-first language is rooted in autistiphobia and anti-autistic bigotry, and its use is widely recognized by most of the autistic community as being a reliable indicator of autistiphobic attitudes. The reason that person-first language is so prevalent in our society's discourses on autism is that those discourses have always been dominated by the voices and viewpoints of autistiphobic bigots. From the 1930s through the present day, the vast majority of the non-autistic people who've written about autism or done any sort of autism-related work have held deeply ingrained autistiphobic attitudes. The language used in their work reflects those attitudes.

The use of person-first language when talking about autistic people is so prevalent and so widely accepted that most non-autistic folks don't think twice about it and don't even recognize it as the language of bigotry and stigma. The autistiphobic bigotry inherent in person-first language doesn't become obvious until you listen to how it sounds when you use that same sort of language to talk about members of other historically oppressed and marginalized groups.

Here, give it a try: *People with homosexuality*? *Children who have Jewishness*? *Adults experiencing femaleness?* Ooh, how about *individuals living with Blackness*? Are you comfortable with those phrases? If you read an article in which the author consistently referred to gay people as *people with homosexuality*, *adults who have homosexuality*, and *individuals living with homosexuality*, what would be your impression of that author's attitude toward being gay?

•

There are only two kinds of people who use person-first language when talking about autistics:

1. Autistiphobic bigots. In other words, people who believe

that there's something wrong with being autistic—that being autistic is in some way a bad thing or a shameful thing.

2. People who don't know any better. In other words, people who picked up the habit of using person-first language because it's so ubiquitous in the discourse on autism (thanks to the influence of autistiphobic bigots), and who've just never really thought enough about the implications of person-first language to recognize its intrinsically autistiphobic nature.

It's generally a waste of time to argue with bigots, whether it's about autistiphobic language or any other issue, because bigots don't argue in good faith. Since they're driven by fear and hatred of difference rather than by reason, they'll just double down and keep repeating the same spurious arguments—or resort to personal attacks, condescension, tone policing, or whatever other derailing tactic they can come up with—rather than acknowledge a valid counterargument.

So I'm writing this essay primarily for the benefit of those who fall into the second category: those who don't know any better, or at least didn't know any better up until now. If you were honestly unaware that person-first language is autistiphobic and that the majority of autistic people these days consider it objectionable—well, that's nothing to be ashamed of. Given the sheer pervasiveness of autistiphobic attitudes and autistiphobic language in the world today, and given that person-first language is even taught in college classrooms and professional training programs, you can hardly be blamed for having accepted and adopted such language without realizing that it's autistiphobic and disrespectful of autistic people. You're not a bad person for not having known any better than what you were taught. And now that you do know better, you can *do* better. You can stop using person-first language and just call autistic people autistic, instead of continuing to inadvertently disrespect and stigmatize us.

The big lie that autistiphobic bigots tell about person-first language is that person-first language is the "respectful" way to talk about autistic people. There's a specific set of spurious arguments that autistiphobic bigots use to support this lie, or to justify their continued use of person-first language when autistic people and our allies object to it. If you were taught to use person-first language when talking about autistic people, chances are that you were also taught to accept these arguments. You may have heard these arguments from people in positions of authority, or from people who supposedly had some sort of expertise on the topic—and as a result, you might have accepted them without giving them the necessary critical scrutiny. So let's do that critical scrutiny right here and now. Let's look at the three most common arguments for person-first language, one by one, and debunk them.

•

Spurious Argument #1: "Person-first language is more respectful because it separates the person from the autism."

No. This is exactly why person-first language is *dis*respectful of autistic people.

Who would want to "separate the person from the autism"? Only someone who believes, deep down, that there's something wrong with being autistic—someone who believes that being autistic in some way a bad thing or a shameful thing. And anyone who believes that it's bad or shameful to be autistic is, by definition, an autistiphobic bigot (just like anyone who believes that it's bad or shameful to be gay is a homophobic bigot, and anyone who believes that it's bad or shameful to be Black is a racist bigot).

Autism doesn't exist separately from autistic people. It's not actually a thing that a person can "have." It isn't a disease, like a tumor or a virus. You can't cut an autism out of a person and preserve it in a bottle. You can't isolate autism in a laboratory and have a little test tube or petri dish full of autism. Being autistic informs every facet of a person's development, embodiment, cognition, and experience, in ways that are pervasive and inseparable from the person's overall being. So the autistic person can't be separated from the autism, and the autism can't be separated from the autistic person.

The idea that an autistic person can be somehow "separated from the autism" is an autistiphobic fantasy. It's a fantasy that appeals to those whose autistiphobia runs so deep that on some level they see being autistic as incompatible with being fully human, and therefore can only see an autistic person as human by pretending that there's a non-autistic version of the person somehow hidden under the autism. Thus, person-first language is born of a fundamental inability or unwillingness to accept autistic people as they are. There's nothing respectful about that.

In fact, person-first language was originally developed by autistiphobic parents of autistic children, and has largely been propagated and insisted upon by such parents—parents who hold the autistiphobic belief that autism is some sort of horrible tragic disorder, and that this disorder functions as a sort of shell under which their imagined "real" (i.e., non-autistic) children are hiding.

These parents are so intensely autistiphobic that they refuse to accept and love the autistic children they actually have, and instead they've constructed a twisted fantasy world in which the terrible disorder of autism has stolen their "real" children from them. According to this fantasy, if parents fight hard enough against autism and steadfastly refuse to accept their autistic children as they are, they might someday magically remove the autism from their children and thus "recover" the non-autistic children that they've wished for all along.

Person-first language was expressly intended to promote and reinforce this sick autistiphobic fantasy, and that's still the primary purpose that person-first language ultimately serves. There are multi-billion-dollar industries today that have been created specifically to exploit this fantasy for profit. These industries include the "autism charity" industry (comprised of money-grubbing "charitable" organizations that raise funds by portraying the existence of autistic children as a heart-rending tragedy), the "behavioral therapy" industry (comprised of providers of bogus "therapies" like ABA, in which autistic children are abused, coerced, and traumatized into imitating the outward behavior of neurotypical children, at the expense of their long-term psychological well-being), and the vast industry of quack pseudo-medical "autism cures" (many of which cause lasting physical and psychological harm, sometimes fatal harm, to the children on which they're inflicted). These industries all harm autistic people and defraud the families of autistic people, while encouraging the "recovery" fantasy and fanning the flames of autistiphobia.

Every time you use person-first language, you're complicit in all of this. I'm sure that's not your intention, but actual impact matters more than naïve good intentions. Every time you use person-first language, you're helping to promote and reinforce a twisted and hateful autistiphobic fantasy. Every time you use person-first language, you're helping to legitimize the industries which profit by exploiting that fantasy—and thus you're complicit in the harm that these industries do to autistic people.

And there's definitely nothing respectful about *that*.

•

Spurious Argument #2: "We have to put the person first to show that they're people first and that autism doesn't define them."

This is just straight-up nonsense. The whole debate about whether to say "autistic person" or (ugh) "person with autism" originated in English-speaking countries and has continued to rage primarily in English-speaking countries. And in the English language, it's standard grammar to place the adjective before the noun.

Anyone fluent in the English language implicitly understands that the noun is primary regardless of where it's placed in relation to the adjective. It's understood that any adjectives placed before the noun merely serve to provide further information about the noun. When I write about a blue Norwegian parrot, for instance, anyone fluent in English understands that it's first and foremost a parrot, and that its color and nationality are secondary to its parrotness.

Anyone fluent the English language also understands that adjectives aren't exclusive—in other words, the presence of a given adjective before a noun doesn't imply that it's the one adjective that entirely and exclusively defines that noun. When I refer to a parrot as "the blue parrot," everyone understands that I'm not in any way implying that the parrot is entirely and exclusively defined by its blueness. Everyone understands that the parrot can be blue and also Norwegian, male, large, resting, and all manner of other things at the same time.

The autistiphobic bigots who react to the phrase "autistic people" with indignant shouts of "Their autism doesn't define them!" are perfectly aware of how adjectives work in English. When you say "six-year-old children," these bigots never jump in with shouts of "Their age doesn't define them!" When you say "tall people" they never jump in with "Their height doesn't define them!" They don't demand that you say "children who are six years old," or "people living with tallness." So the argument that we have to use person-first language in order to affirm that autistic people are "people first" and that "autism doesn't define them" is not only downright ridiculous, it's also disingenuous.

The real reason these people insist on person-first language, and the real reason they freak out when people use the adjective "autistic" the same way one would use any other adjective, is autistiphobia. Deep down, because of their own unresolved psychological issues, they fear and despise autistic people. But because they need to convince themselves of their own goodness, they can't admit to themselves that they feel such fear and hatred toward a group of people—especially not a group which, in the case of many autistiphobes, might include their own children.

So instead, they buy into the autistiphobic fantasy already discussed: the fantasy that the autism can somehow be separated from the person. This enables them to pretend that it's only some horrid "disorder" or "condition" called autism toward which they feel aversion, rather than actual autistic human beings. It's exactly the same strategy of self-deception that homophobic right-wing Christian bigots use when they pretend that they don't hate gay people and instead just hate "the sin of homosexuality."

When a person relies on denial and fantasy to protect their own psyche from deeply uncomfortable truths, the arrangement is fragile. Anything that contradicts the fantasy threatens to bring the whole thing crashing down, and threatens to bring the person face to face with the realities they're so desperately hiding from themselves. If they were to accept even for a moment that the autism can't ever be separated from the autistic person, they'd have to face an overwhelming flood of deeply uncomfortable repressed feelings and repressed truths (including, in the case of many autistiphobic parents, the truth that they've been unable to accept and love the person their autistic child actually is).

This is why so many autistiphobes don't just insist on using person-first language, but also aggressively insist that everyone else should use person-first language, too. The fantasy is so fragile, and their need to keep hiding reality from themselves is so strong, that even hearing the phrase "autistic person" feels like an existential threat to them on some visceral unconscious level.

They can't look at where their strong feelings and reactions are truly coming from (since that would involve looking at their own denial), so instead they come up with desperate rationalizations to justify those feelings and reactions. And that's how they end up making such a patently absurd argument as "We have to put the person first to show that they're people first and that autism doesn't define them"—an argument which, as we've now seen, makes no sense, given how adjectives actually work in the English language.

So once again, we find that person-first language has nothing to do with being respectful of autistic people. As previously noted, the fantasy that person-first language serves to promote—the fantasy that autism can be separated from an autistic person—is a fantasy that exists for the comfort of autistiphobes, and has dire consequences for autistic people. So using person-first language is in fact grossly disrespectful of autistic people, because it prioritizes the fantasies and fragilities of autistiphobes over autistic well-being.

•

Spurious Argument #3: "I'm a trained professional [or I've listened to professionals] and person-first language is what I was taught to use; it's standard in the field."

We live in a profoundly autistiphobic society in which the discourses on autism, including the academic and professional discourses, have been dominated from the beginning by autistiphobic voices and viewpoints. The reason that person-first language is the standard in whatever academic or professional fields you're involved in (or in the academic and professional fields of whatever non-autistic "experts" you've learned about autism from) is that autistiphobia is deeply ingrained in the history, literature, conventions, and practices of those fields. This applies to fields as disparate as psychology, medicine, education, social work, journalism, and neurobiology (and if you think a physical science like biology can't have bigotry ingrained in it, go look up "scientific racism").

The professors, professionals, and other "experts" who taught you to use person-first language were either autistiphobic bigots themselves, or else were well-intentioned but ill-informed people who learned from the work of autistiphobic bigots and passed the autistiphobic language and lessons along to the next generation without recognizing them as harmful.

So please, never say anything like "Person-first language is what I was taught to use," unless it's the first half of a sentence and the second half is something along the lines of "but now I know better and will never use it again." Believe me, autistic people already know quite well that person-first language is what you were taught to use. We already know that you learned about autism from autistiphobic bigots, or from people who uncritically passed along the harmful lessons of autistiphobic bigots. We already know that autistiphobic bigotry is deeply ingrained in whatever academic or professional fields you've turned to for knowledge in the past. You don't need to remind us of any of this. We don't want to hear your attempts to justify your use of autistiphobic language. We're not asking you to explain yourself, we're asking you to start doing better.

Your society is autistiphobic. Your field is autistiphobic. Your "experts" are autistiphobic. Your teachers were autistiphobic. We're asking you to be better and to do better. Doing better means recognizing that many things you were taught about autistic people were just plain wrong, and that much of the language that you were taught was acceptable or preferable to use when speaking about us— including person-first language—is actually stigmatizing, insulting, and harmful to us. Doing better means refusing to perpetuate the autistiphobic language, beliefs, and practices that you were taught, even when that refusal puts you at odds with the authorities and traditions from which you've previously learned.

•

Every autistic person who spends any significant length of time working to combat autistiphobia within public, academic, or professional spheres—especially if any of their work takes place on social media—eventually learns an ironic truth: the non-autistics who are most insistent on using person-first language when talking about us, the ones who most loudly declare that person-first language is more "respectful" because "it puts the person first," *always* turn out to be the ones who have the least respect for us and who don't really see us as people at all.

In two decades of autism-related advocacy, teaching, and scholarship, I've found this correlation between autistiphobic bigotry and person-first language to be a 100 percent reliable constant. It's a truth widely recognized within the autistic community these days. Most of us know that we can never trust a person-firster, and those who don't learn this lesson through observation or by listening to fellow autistics end up learning the hard way sooner or later.

A lot of autistiphobes who've been called out for using person-first language have tried to dodge the whole issue by using euphemisms like "on the spectrum" as another way to avoid saying "autistic." Guess what? We autistics see exactly what you're doing. We're notoriously good at pattern recognition. Whether it's person-first language or euphemisms, we can tell when someone is trying desperately to avoid just calling us autistic. And we know that the refusal to just call autistic people autistic is the universally reliable number one sign that someone is an autistiphobic bigot.

As I explained earlier in this essay, the refusal to call autistic people autistic is often a sign that a person's autistiphobia is so intense that they've sought refuge in the desperate fantasy that the autism can be separated from the person. And of course, calling an autistic person autistic is an acknowledgement of reality that threatens to bring this whole pathetic fragile fantasy crashing down.

Any doubts I may have had about the accuracy of this explanation have been dispelled by the results of an experiment that I like to perform when I give trainings on autism to groups of psychotherapists, social workers, special ed teachers, or other professionals. The experiment is simple: one by one, I have each participant look me in the eyes and say to me, "You are autistic."

I'm not a big fan of eye contact, but in this case it's worth it. The autistiphobia of many of the participants is instantly exposed, and it also becomes quite evident just how desperately they're clinging to their pitiful autistiphobic fantasy that we're "people with autism" rather than autistic people.

You see, it turns out that when I ask these adult professionals to look me in the eye and acknowledge out loud that I'm autistic, many of them just can't do it. They squirm. They look down and avoid my gaze. They argue and bargain and complain. Some of them shut down completely. Some of them fly into indignant rages and storm out of the room. A lot of them cry. One time, one of them threw up. Autistiphobia runs deep, and its connection to the terms people use to talk about us should not be underestimated.

A person who can't just call autistic people autistic is a person autistic people can't trust, and a person who should never ever be permitted to be in a position of any authority over autistic people or to work with autistic people in any professional capacity.

If you're a non-autistic person who's accustomed to using person-first language or euphemisms, put yourself to the test. Start calling autistic people autistic. If it's easy for you to make the switch to calling us autistic, that's excellent. You're now one more voice refusing to perpetuate autistiphobic language and the autistiphobic attitudes and fantasies associated with such language. Thank you.

And if it's hard for you to discard the person-first language and the evasive euphemisms? If it's hard for you to start calling us autistic? If you find yourself resisting the change, making excuses, having trouble just saying or writing the phrase "autistic people"? Well, now you've learned something important about yourself, and you have some work to do.

On the Practice of Stimming

When I was writing my doctoral dissertation, I needed to include a definition of stimming. I couldn't find one that satisfied me, so I wrote my own from scratch. In case anyone else also has use for a good definition of stimming, here it is. I wrote the original dissertation version of this piece sometime in 2018. The version I'm sharing here has been newly revised to enable it to better stand on its own and to make it a bit more readable.

A major defining feature of autistic embodiment is the tendency to engage in repetitive physical movements or other actions that provide specific forms of sensory stimulation. In conventional disciplinary discourses on autism based in the pathology paradigm, such actions have traditionally been referred to as *stereotypy* or *self-stimulatory behavior*, and are regarded as pathological symptoms that are best eliminated. In a crucial step toward taking back ownership of narratives about autistic embodiment, autistics transformed the pathologizing and rather ungainly term *self-stimulatory behavior* into the more graceful and less medical-sounding term *stimming*. The root word *stim* functions as both a verb and a noun: "I stim by rocking back and forth; rocking back and forth is my favorite stim."

The infinite possible varieties of stimming include, but are certainly not limited to:

- *proprioceptive* or *kinesthetic* (e.g., rocking, pacing, waving or flapping one's hands, seeking physical pressure or impact);

- *tactile* (e.g., touching objects and surfaces with appealing textures, stroking one's own skin);

- *vestibular* (e.g., spinning or swinging);

- *visual* (e.g., gazing at running water or rising smoke);

- *auditory* (e.g., listening to running water or loud music);

- *olfactory* or *gustatory* (e.g., sniffing or tasting things);

- *verbal* (e.g., repetition of particular words or phrases);

- any combination of the above (e.g., drumming, which combines the kinesthetic, the tactile, and the auditory).

Pathology-oriented discourse around autism has tended to frame stimming as dysfunctional compulsive or automatic behavior that serves no purpose other than to detract from an autistic person's performance of normativity—the performance of normativity being, from the perspective of those operating within the pathology paradigm, the goal toward which all autistics should be relentlessly pushed regardless of their own needs or wishes. The majority of autistics, on the other hand, along with a growing number of non-autistic thinkers who've come to view autism and autistics from perspectives less bound by the assumptions of the pathology paradigm, recognize stimming as serving vital functions in autistic consciousness.

Among those researchers and professionals who recognize that it has value and purpose, stimming is most commonly understood as serving essential functions of self-regulation and integration—that is, as being a means by which autistics are able to regulate their chaotic experience to avoid being overwhelmed by it, and by which they are able to better integrate that experience in order to bring increased coherence and navigability to their perceptual worlds. Non-autistic infants in what Jean Piaget called the *sensorimotor stage* of development, immersed in the developmental task of parsing the blooming, buzzing confusion of the sensory field into coherence, are constantly engaged in stimming, even though it's not commonly referred to as stimming when non-autistic infants do it. Given the central role of stimming in the developmental task of parsing and integrating the sensory field, and given that parsing and integrating the sensory field tends to be more of an ongoing lifelong activity for autistics rather than just an early developmental stage, it makes sense that stimming would also be a lifelong activity for autistics.

While stimming does indeed serve these vital regulatory and integrative functions for autistics, an understanding of stimming that looks no further than those particular functions is woefully incomplete. Such an understanding is of course a vast improvement over the conventional view of stimming as a purposeless and pathological symptom to be eradicated—but it is nonetheless a limited understanding, and I suspect the limitations derive from the same paternalistic attitudes and implicit assumptions of neurotypical superiority that lie at the root of the pathology paradigm.

When stimming is understood as *only* a coping strategy or accommodation that enables autistics to compensate for their alleged neurobiological or sensorimotor "defects," the underlying narrative is still a narrative in which autistics are defective—a narrative which implicitly assumes that the only worthwhile potential of autistics is their potential to compensate for their putative defects well enough to fit into neurotypical society and be almost-normal, and a narrative that thus implicitly dismisses the possibility that there are autistic capacities and potentials worth exploring that have nothing to do with aspiring to normativity or with mere compensation.

Discussions of stimming in the first-hand accounts of autistics offer a striking contrast to this reductionist narrative. In some first-person accounts of autistic experience (particularly among autistics who have liberated themselves from disempowering narratives of pathology), stimming is revealed to be a highly complex and sophisticated body of intuitive sensorimotor practices. In addition to serving to regulate and integrate sensory, perceptual, cognitive, and emotional experience, stimming can also function as a way of exploring and relating to the sensory world, and as a means of accessing not only a wide range of cognitive and emotional capacities but also exceptional human capacities such as flow states or experiences of profound communion and ego transcendence.

It's worth noting here that the act of stimulating one's own senses in specific ways in order to access certain states, feelings, or capacities is hardly unique to autistics. Everyone does this to some degree, in some way or other. Every day, millions of neurotypical individuals engage in such behaviors as pacing back and forth because it helps them think, drumming their fingers on a desk or table, pausing to deeply inhale a pleasing scent, letting themselves be soothed and entranced by the sound of rain on the roof or the sight of flickering flames in a fireplace, stroking a pet or the hair or skin of a lover because it feels good, or spontaneously moving their bodies as they get into the groove of a piece of music. One could therefore argue that everybody stims, and that autistics, because stimming is such an essential practice for the regulation and navigation of autistic sensory and cognitive experience, simply tend to stim more than non-autistics.

Based on the origins and common usage of the term *stim*, however, I would argue that the sort of activities described in the previous paragraph, as ordinarily performed by neurotypical individuals, are properly excluded from the category of stimming by virtue of the very fact that they fall within the commonly accepted neurotypical norms of behavior and embodiment. Such activities, when engaged in by neurotypical individuals, are not commonly regarded as symptoms of any dire pathology, nor assigned such labels such as "self-stimulatory behavior," because they fall within the bounds of dominant cultural standards of neuronormativity. I would argue that in some way and at least to some small degree, an action must necessarily fall outside the bounds of neuronormative performance in order to qualify as stimming.

With all this in mind, I offer the following as a working definition: *To stim is to engage in any action that falls outside the boundaries of the social performance of normativity, and that provides some form of sensory stimulation in order to facilitate, intentionally or otherwise, some particular cognitive or sensorimotor process, or access to some particular state or capacity of consciousness or sensorimotor experience.*

The Story Behind "This Is Autism"

On November 11th, 2013, a large and well-funded anti-autistic hate group—an organization ironically named "Autism Speaks," which boasts an extensive history of promoting the stigmatization, silencing, disenfranchisement, abuse, murder, and eugenic extermination of autistic people—released a "call for action" authored by one of its founders.

Like much of the previous anti-autistic hate speech produced by Autism Speaks, this "call for action" characterized the very existence of autistic children as a "monumental health crisis" a "national emergency," and a terrible, life-destroying tragedy visited upon the families of these children. As is usual in the rhetoric of Autism Speaks, the existence of millions of autistic adults was not mentioned at all; acknowledging our existence would make it hard for them to keep selling the lie that autism is a growing "epidemic" rather than a manifestation of human biodiversity which serves an evolutionary purpose and has most likely been present in the species since our hunter-gatherer origins.

Written in the tone of over-the-top alarmism characteristic of the rhetoric of hate groups everywhere, this hand-wringing "call for action" featured melodramatic descriptions of the daily horrors allegedly faced by parents of autistic children. Three times, in the course of this list of horrors, the author repeated the sentence "This is autism" in bold lettering for extra dramatic effect.

Unsurprisingly, the autistic community took issue with this. A week later, on November 18th, an autistic blogger named Cynthia Kim organized a flash blog as a creative pushback. A flash blog is when a whole bunch of people all make blog posts on a single topic on the same day; I don't know whether this is still a thing that anyone does, but it was a thing people did back in 2013. An impressive number of autistics and allies wrote things for the flash blog, and the piece that follows, predictably entitled "This Is Autism," was my contribution. Its original 2013 publication date makes it one of the oldest pieces in this book; the only one that predates it is "Throw Away the Master's Tools."

Since the original piece of Autism Speaks hate speech that inspired the flash blog featured a series of brief melodramatic depictions of the horrors of living with autistic children, I figured I'd make my piece a series of brief accurate depictions of my experiences being autistic and meeting up with other autistic folks.

The version of "This Is Autism" that appears here has been edited a bit from the original. In the original version, I spoofed the melodramatic Autism Speaks "call for action" piece by putting the sentence "This is autism" in bold lettering in between scenes, just like the Autism Speaks founder had done. I took it out in this version because I think my piece reads better without it; the satirical boldface "This is autism" refrain only made sense in the piece's original context. I also cut out a couple of scenes that just don't work as well for me anymore, for one reason or another.

The Autism Speaks co-founder who wrote the original "call for action" died in 2016. As soon as she was gone, Autism Speaks began a major rebranding. They continued supporting the disenfranchisement, abuse, murder, and eugenic extermination of autistic people, but they toned down their rhetoric to make their agenda a good deal less obvious to the uninformed observer. Autistic activist efforts like that flash blog had started to put a dent in their popularity and their bottom line—a small dent, but apparently enough to make them realize that times were a-changin' and that it would be better for business if they made an effort to look and sound like something other than the hate group they are. As part of their rebranding, they took down that melodramatic "call for action" hate piece by their departed co-founder. So my "This Is Autism" piece has long outlasted the dreadful bit of garbage that first inspired it.

This Is Autism

It's a bright cool Sunday in Berkeley, and when I step into my aikido dojo the sun is singing through the skylights, suffusing the big airy space and making shiny hot pools of white on the rich vibrant blue of the mat. That vibrant expanse of blue makes a low soft thrumming and gives me a feeling of warm wide open spaces behind me and in the lower part of my lungs. The sunlight sounds like a choir of angels, and together with the pleasantly humming mint-flavored whiteness of walls it makes my skin tingle and opens a luminous sky in my chest and all around my head. I inhale into that space and the cool air fills my head with exhilarating white-blue and brings new, higher harmonies into the choir.

There's a moment of silence waiting for me at the top of the inhale, and just as I reach it I realize that another sound is happening, too, a grey-brown sound that rolls and tumbles like an otter in the blue-white river of sensation. This sound is incongruous and merits investigation, so as I begin to breathe out I do that trick that I learned to do when I was a real tiny kid, the trick that no one ever talked about and that I could never explain to anyone because, as I eventually learned long after I grew up, for most people it's not a trick that they have to do, it's just the way they are all the time. The trick where I filter and sort and separate the currents of the river until they resolve themselves into a world of discrete objects with names and meanings.

Dojo, walls, blue mat on blonde wood floor. Seven of my aikido students in white gi, early arrivals for class, on the mat, stretching. The choir is still singing blue-white, the walls still have that minty tingle. Interpreting some of the currents and eddies of the river as discrete objects with names doesn't make the river stop. The flow is always happening. The world of discrete objects and names is a part of the river, too, and it's the part where most other people live by default. Me, I'm just visiting.

Once I've made the necessary shift in consciousness, it becomes clear to me that the grey-brown tumbling otter sound that got my attention was someone talking to me. A greeting, I think, from one of the students on the mat. Yes, he's looking at me.

Quick mental checklist, made quicker by the fact that I don't think in words and thus don't have to go through it in a linear fashion. If it were a literal checklist, though, written out in words, it would go something like this:

Does his greeting call for a response on my part? Yes, definitely.

Is he smiling? Yes.

Should I smile back? Yes.

Do I already happen to be smiling? Yes. How convenient!

Does this exchange of greetings also require speech on my part? Most likely.

Have I now taken so long to respond that there may be some potential social awkwardness to navigate? Probably not. In terms of clock time it's only been a couple of seconds. A slightly longer pause than is usual for the ordinary rhythms of social conversation, but my students are quite accustomed to my pauses by now.

"Good Morning," I say, smiling.

I bow, because I'm entering the dojo, and one bows when one enters the dojo.

It's past noon by the clock, but I say *Good Morning* because I always say *Good Morning*. Yet another quirk to which my students are well accustomed.

I like to remember that it's always morning *somewhere*.

•

Julia and Zoe come to town. We meet on the porch of a Thai restaurant near my apartment in North Berkeley. Julia is taller than I expected. It is my intention to have Thai food for lunch, but Julia has not experienced Thai food and is reluctant to do so at this time.

There was a long period in my adolescence and young adulthood when I would have regarded Julia's reluctance to eat Thai food as something that I should help her to overcome, by badgering her in the manner that I learned as a child from Sam I Am in Dr. Seuss' *Green Eggs and Ham*. "Would you eat them in a box? Would you eat them with a fox?"

Now, though, my years of immersion in the emergent autistic culture have deeply inculcated in me a rule that I think of as the Golden Rule of Neurodiversity: *Respect the bodily, sensory, and cognitive needs of others as you would want your own to be respected, whether or not you understand the reasons for those needs.*

So I suggest an establishment across the street, that serves good cuisine of a more Euro-American variety. A place where Julia and Zoe can have pancakes with whipped cream for lunch, while I can have a large salad with some sort of spicy ginger dressing that satisfies my own sensory preferences. The noise and bad acoustics inside this establishment are unpleasant for all three of us, so we elect to sit at a table out on the sidewalk. Julia has found a small purplish flower somewhere, and she twirls, twirls, twirls it between her thumb and forefinger while we wait for our food. We all watch the flower, watch it spin, spin, spin.

•

Kassiane comes to town. We lunch on delicious Thai food, on the porch of a Thai restaurant near my apartment in North Berkeley.

I've been reading Kassiane's activist writings online for more than a dozen years. Her writing is fiery and powerful, the writing of someone who has learned well and truly that the consequences of standing up and pushing back hard against the forces of oppression are never as bad as the consequences of *not* pushing back. I know a lot of people who are scared of her. I regard her as a hero.

In person, Kassiane is smaller that I expected, and she has a white cat named Purkinje who rides on her shoulder. She looks ten years younger than her age, and her voice is soft and light, easy on the ears. She loves the color purple. I've seen photos of her with purple hair, but today it's brown. She might or might not be wearing purple. I can't tell. It doesn't matter. Because everything she does is a beautiful bright purple. My brain processes her voice as purple, her movements as purple. She's warm and friendly, and when she hugs me, she means it, and I feel like I've been enveloped by a purple glow.

•

Riki comes to town. She knows the species, traits, and potential uses of every plant in the neighborhood. She smells of patchouli and walks with a cane, and my daughter loves her.

Riki spends hours fixing my out-of-commission electric scooter, taking it apart and putting it back together. It seems to me that she's doing me a great favor working on my scooter, but from Riki's perspective, I'm doing *her* a favor because she's never had the opportunity to take this sort of scooter apart before. The whole time she works on the scooter, she talks to it like she's a friendly veterinarian talking to an animal. She refuses to take a break to eat.

Afterward, I take her out for Thai food.

•

The youngest and most enthusiastic student in my aikido dojo, the girl is five years old and so small that even the smallest size of gi is adorably large on her.

She *loves* aikido. Like me, when I started my own aikido training at the age of twelve, she has a hard time learning the moves, but she keeps on working at it because she gets what the art is about, she appreciates its sublime beauty in a way that most people, so far as I can tell, don't arrive at until they've been training for ten or twenty or thirty years.

That's my secret, really. The secret to how I ended up as the senior instructor of a thriving aikido dojo. Most people assume that I had some sort of natural physical talent for it, but nothing could be further from the truth. The secret was that the beauty of the art touched me, that I could see from the beginning that its dance contained all the sublime subtle grace that I saw and loved in the flight of birds and the movement of the ocean's waves. And even though I had no talent for the art at all, I wanted so much to feel what it was like to embody that grace, that I was willing to put in as much work as I had to in order to get there.

More than three decades later, I'm still at it; I've gotten far enough now that I've had some first tastes of that grace, now and then in recent years, and it's just served to whet my appetite.

This little girl can see the beauty, too. And today, before class starts, she can barely wait to talk to me. But she still remembers to stop and bow when she enters the dojo.

After her bow, she comes bounding across the mat to me.

"Hello, Sensei," she says.

"Good Morning," I say.

"Today is a special class!" She informs me, looking somewhere past my left shoulder. "Today is my fifty-third aikido class!"

"Ah," I say. I think for just a moment, then it comes to me. "That's a prime, isn't it?"

"Yes!" she laughs, and bounds away across the blue mat, hands flapping.

Comments on "This Is Autism"

In 2012, while researching the massive tome that he would publish in 2015 under the title *NeuroTribes*, my friend Steve Silberman visited my dojo and watched me teach an aikido class. After the class was over, Steve interviewed me over dinner at the same Thai restaurant that's featured in "This Is Autism."

At one point during out conversation, he remarked, "I think the way you do aikido has got to be the most sophisticated form of stimming I've ever seen."

"Exactly what I've been going for," I said.

•

The Julia who appears in "This Is Autism" is the same one who put together the *Loud Hands* anthology for which I wrote the first version of "Throw Away the Master's Tools." In fact, the meeting described in "This Is Autism" was the 2011 meeting at which we discussed *Loud Hands* and I agreed to write something about the neurodiversity paradigm for it.

•

The Kassiane who appears in "This Is Autism" is, of course, Kassiane Asasumasu, who's mentioned a few times in this book because she coined the terms *neurodivergent* and *neurodivergence*. The moment described here was our first in-person meeting but not our last. She remains a friend, and dear to my heart. Sometime after "This Is Autism" was written, Kassiane began training at an aikido dojo in her own hometown, joining the distinguished ranks of autistic aikido practitioners.

•

The Riki who appears in "This Is Autism" is my friend Riki Sarah Dennis. We're both transgender autistic women and we went through the Transformative Studies doctoral program at California Institute of Integral Studies together. At the time of the visit recounted in "This Is Autism," she'd only recently figured out she was autistic and I hadn't yet figured out I was a woman. I supported her as best I could through her process of coming out as autistic, and a few years later she supported me as best she could through my process of coming out as transgender.

•

These days my wife Azzia runs the youth program at our aikido dojo, and we both teach the adults. In both the youth classes and the adult classes, the majority of our students aren't autistic, though at any given time we have at least a couple who are.

Which brings me to this word of advice I'd like to offer to parents of autistic kids, or any other adults with autistic kids in their care, who are considering aikido training or training in some other martial art as a way to support the kids' long-term empowerment and well-being: please note that absolutely *none* of my aikido training has occurred in the context of any sort of "special" program or class designed specifically with autistics in mind. I began my aikido training in classes in which I was the only autistic participant. All of my training since then has occurred in settings that were not in an way designed for autistics, and in which either I was the only autistic or in which there were a couple of other autistics but we were still considerably in the minority.

I wouldn't have had it any other way. From everything I've seen, programs of activity designed specially for autistics (at least when non-autistics have a hand in their design or implementation) seem to inevitably tend toward the paternalistic, toward condescension and lowered expectations, and toward incorporating and insidiously prioritizing agendas of normativity. There has been no time in my life at which I would have voluntarily subjected myself to the indignity of such a program; had I been forced to participate in one in my youth, my energies would have been focused entirely on resisting it and seeking to extricate myself. If my exposure to aikido had occurred in the context of such a program, instead of among non-autistic fellow students in a traditional dojo environment with the traditional goals, expectations, and teaching methodology, I wouldn't have stuck with aikido and it's unlikely that I'd be thriving as I am today.

When it comes to fostering autistic well-being through practices like martial arts, dance, theater, or what-have-you, the best long-term outcomes for autistics are achieved not through putting them in segregated "special" programs (ugh), but through their voluntary participation in systems and communities of practice in which they work side-by-side with their non-autistic fellow practitioners with no agenda except to work toward mastery of the practice for its own sake. That's how I did my training, and that's how we do it in my dojo today.

For Parents of Autistic Children

This one was originally written in 2015 as the foreword to a book of short writings by autistic authors, compiled for parents of autistic children. That book is out of print now, and my foreword seems worth re-publishing here. It's a nice little beginner-friendly piece and it's one of the few things I've written so far that's specifically addressed to non-autistic parents of autistic children.

Every good and loving parent in the world faces the same question every day: *How do I help my child to thrive?*

Every time a truly good and loving parent makes any sort of parenting choice, however big or small—whether it's choosing a school or choosing a bedtime story, choosing when to put a toddler down for a nap or choosing what rules and advice to give a teen about dating—that is the question we must answer as best we can, the question that guides our decisions, even if we never put it into words. *How do I help my child to thrive?*

Any good parent can tell you that this question is endlessly challenging. No matter how many times we grapple with it and find what we hope is a good answer, a new situation is guaranteed to come along soon that requires us to grapple with it yet again and to find yet another answer. And sometimes we have to wait months or years or even decades to find out how good our answers were.

If your child is autistic, and you're not autistic yourself, the question of how to help your child to thrive becomes a hundred times harder. But this is *not* because being autistic is in any way incompatible with thriving. Rest assured that autistic people *can* thrive, and *do* thrive. Autistic people, including your child, can have good lives full of joy and love and meaningful connection and creative fulfillment.

So why *is* it so hard to determine how to help your autistic child to thrive? Most of the difficulty can be traced to three factors. The first factor is that your child's sensory experience of the world is fundamentally different from yours, and the way your child's mind works is fundamentally different from yours. So different that it may be nigh-impossible for you to imagine what your child experiences, senses, thinks, knows, or feels, or what your child is trying to communicate, or why your child is doing some particular thing . And this, of course, can make it quite difficult to figure out what your child needs. Fortunately, the insights of autistic adults can be of great help in this regard. Autistic adults have been there. They have insider knowledge.

The second factor is that there's so much misinformation and bad advice about autism out there. Many of the standard "expert" or "professional" approaches to autism are badly misguided and rooted in ignorance. For instance, there are certain "therapies" that are widely recommended for autistic children but that are actually harmful and traumatizing. When so many of the "experts" are so utterly wrong and so confident in their prejudices and misinformation, it's hard to know who to listen to. Here, again, the insights and insider knowledge of autistic adults are invaluable.

The third factor is that because the minds, interests, experiences, abilities, and needs of autistic people are different from those of non-autistic people, thriving also looks different in autistic people than it does in non-autistic people. Health, happiness, success, personal fulfillment, good relationships, psychological well-being, a high quality of life—all of these things are possible for autistic people, including your child, but the autistic versions of these things are often quite different from the non-autistic versions.

When you're trying to help a "typical" child to thrive, the society in which you live provides you with many models of what a thriving child looks like, and many models of successful, thriving adulthood. These models provide some idea of what you're aiming for, some idea of what you want to help your child to become. But parents rarely have access to models of what a thriving *autistic* child looks like, or a successful, thriving autistic adult. So how do you know if your autistic child is on the right track, developmentally, when the "right track" for your child might be vastly different from the established societal standards of what the right track looks like?

Most non-autistic "experts" are unhelpful about this sort of thing, because they regard autism as intrinsically unhealthy, intrinsically a "wrong track." Most non-autistic "experts" think that key to helping an autistic person thrive is to try to make them non-autistic, or to try to make them as indistinguishable from a non-autistic person as possible. Making an autistic person into a non-autistic person simply can't be done (though sadly, many parents fall prey to unscrupulous quacks and cultish organizations selling phony and expensive "treatments" for autism). And trying to make an autistic person outwardly indistinguishable from a non-autistic person ultimately does the autistic person far more harm than good.

So when it comes to the question of what the path to a good life might look like for your autistic child, autistic adults can yet again offer crucial insight, and can also serve as examples of what's possible.

Most of us had a hard time getting to the point where we were thriving, and many of us are still recovering from the hard times we had. We want the next generation of autistic children, including your child, to have an easier time. Like you, we want your child to thrive.

Autism and the Pathology Paradigm

This little essay started out as an excerpt from my doctoral dissertation proposal. In 2016 I revised it so that it would stand well enough on its own, and posted it on the Neurocosmopolitanism website. It's written in formal enough language that quotes from it can fit nicely into academic papers, so it's one of those pieces that a lot of students and academic-types have found useful.

Discourse and education on autism, in the academic and professional realms, has thus far been dominated by what I have termed the *pathology paradigm*. At the root of the pathology paradigm is the assumption that there is one "right" style of human neurocognitive functioning. Variations in neurocognitive functioning that diverge substantially from socially constructed standards of "normal"—including the variations that constitute autism—are framed within this paradigm as medical pathologies, as deficits, damage, or "disorders."

In recent years a new paradigm has begun to emerge, which I refer to as the *neurodiversity paradigm*. The term *neurodiversity,* coined in the 1990s, refers to the diversity of human minds—the variations in neurocognitive functioning that manifest within the human species. Within the neurodiversity paradigm, neurodiversity is understood to be a form of human diversity that is subject to social dynamics—including the dynamics of oppression and systemic social power inequalities—similar to those dynamics that commonly occur around other forms of human diversity such as racial diversity or diversity of gender and sexual orientation.

Through the lens of the neurodiversity paradigm, the pathology paradigm's medicalized framing of autism and various other constellations of neurological, cognitive, and behavioral characteristics as "disorders" or "conditions" can be seen for what it is: a social construction rooted in cultural norms and social power inequalities, rather than a "scientifically objective" description of reality.

The choice to frame the minds, bodies, and lives of autistic people (or any other neurological minority group) in terms of pathology does not represent an inevitable and objective scientific conclusion, but is merely a cultural value judgment. Similar pathologizing frameworks have been used time and again to lend an aura of scientific legitimacy to all manner of other bigotry, and to the oppression of women, indigenous peoples, people of color, and queer people, among others. The framing of autism and other minority neurological configurations as disorders or medical conditions begins to lose its aura of scientific authority and "objectivity" when viewed in this historical context—when one remembers, for instance, that homosexuality was classified as a mental disorder in the American Psychiatric Association's *Diagnostic and Statistical Manual of Mental Disorders* (DSM) well into the 1970s; or that in the Southern United States, for some years prior to the American Civil War, the desire of slaves to escape from slavery was diagnosed by some white Southern physicians as a medical "disorder" called drapetomania.

At this time, sadly, the pathologization of autistic minds, bodies, and lives still has not been widely recognized—especially not within the academic and professional mainstream—as being yet another manifestation of this all-too-familiar form of institutionalized oppression and othering. The academic and professional discourse on autism, and the miseducation on autism given to each new generation of professionals, remain uncritically mired in the assumptions of the pathology paradigm. And since bad assumptions and unexamined prejudices inevitably become self-reinforcing when mistaken for facts, this entrenchment in the pathology paradigm has kept autism-related theory, praxis, and education stuck in a self-perpetuating cycle of ignorance and bigotry.

A proper accounting of the devastating consequences of this ignorance and bigotry, both for autistic persons and for society, would fill many pages and would be beyond the intended scope of this brief essay. However, for the benefit of those readers less familiar with the realm of autism-related professional and institutional praxis, a brief summary of the general shape of the situation is in order. The crux of the matter is that the neurodiversity paradigm is fundamentally in alignment with the social model of disability (disability understood as the result of failures of accommodation, societal attitudes, and systemic barriers, which conflict with the needs, traits, and abilities of specific groups and individuals); whereas the pathology paradigm is inextricably entwined with the medical model of disability (disability attributed exclusively to medicalized defects located within the disabled individual, with the implicit assumption that status quo societal norms are more or less "right" and "natural" and that having traits and needs that are incompatible with those norms constitutes a personal deficiency).

The near-total dominance of the pathology paradigm (and thus of the medical model of disability) in the discourse on autism means that autism-related professional and institutional praxis is overwhelmingly dominated by a focus on "fixing" autistic persons—i.e., trying to make them non-autistic—at the expense of any significant focus on societal acceptance of autism, accommodation of autistic needs, removal of systemic barriers to access and inclusion, or supporting autistic persons in thriving *as* autistic persons. Further, since it is not actually possible to make an autistic person into a non-autistic person, the focus on this goal has inevitably served to generate nothing but absurd pseudoscience, quackery, and horrifying abuses.

The worst and most widespread abuses have been those perpetrated under the guise of "behavioral therapies" (e.g., Applied Behavior Analysis, or ABA), which have been used to torture and traumatize two generations of autistic children, and which remain popular with parents and professionals despite the warnings of autistic adult survivors. The popularity of these abusive "behavioral therapies" can be traced directly to the focus on the impossible goal of making autistic persons into non-autistic persons, a goal implicitly mandated by the pathology paradigm. Behaviorism circumvents the impossibility of this goal by pretending that superficial outward compliance with specified non-autistic behavioral norms is the same thing as "recovery from autism," while ignoring the long-term psychological costs of such compliance and of the abusive methods used to attain it.

The dominance of the pathology paradigm makes the proliferation of such abuses inevitable. Only a fundamental shift in the discourse—a shift from the pathology paradigm to the neurodiversity paradigm—is likely to create any substantial improvement in the realm of autism-related praxis.

Making the Shift to the Neurodiversity Paradigm

In 2020, my esteemed friend and colleague Dora M. Raymaker conducted an extensive interview with me via email which was eventually published in the academic journal Autism in Adulthood (vol. 3, no. 1) in March of 2021 under the title, "Toward a Neuroqueer Future: An Interview with Nick Walker." This piece is a revised version of one brief passage from that interview.

As I see it, the long-term aim of our work is a cultural paradigm shift: a widespread supplanting of the pathology paradigm by the neurodiversity paradigm. For those who want to be a part of making this happen, there's a set of practices we'll need to cultivate rigorously in the years to come.

First, we'll need to be absolutely clear—in our own minds and in our written and spoken discourse—that the pathology paradigm is nothing more than institutionalized bigotry masquerading as science, and that it's illegitimate and harmful in the same sort of ways as racism, misogyny, and other forms of bigotry that have also historically masqueraded as science.

Second, we'll need to train ourselves to recognize the pathology paradigm in all its myriad manifestations. The nature of any culture's dominant paradigms is that they're so pervasive that they become normalized to the point of invisibility for anyone raised within that culture. This is why so many people fail to recognize sexism or racism when it's happening right in front of them. Waking up and learning to see the pathology paradigm is like waking up and learning to see any other form of systemic oppression. When we hear someone refer to autism as a "disorder" or "condition," it should instantly set off the same sort of alarm bells in our minds as hearing someone refer to homosexuality as a "disorder" or refer to a member of some specific ethnic group as "inferior." A pathology paradigm phrase like "individuals with autism" should register with us as inappropriate in the same way that we intuitively recognize that there's something wrong with the phrase "individuals with homosexuality."

Third, we'll need to get a lot better about holding the boundary that the pathology paradigm is every bit as unacceptable as any other form of bigotry. And yes, this means rejecting almost all autism-related discourse and research produced over the past 90 years or so. I'm all for that. Up until the 1970s, nearly all scholarship pertaining to homosexuality framed it as a mental disorder, and professional practice was geared toward figuring out its causes, treating it, and/or preventing it. Sound familiar? In 1960, it would've been unthinkable to most psychologists to throw out every bit of scholarship and practice that stigmatized homosexuality and treated it as a pathology. And yet, over the past few decades, the academic and professional mainstream has done exactly that—and the results have been entirely beneficial.

Today, if a psychology professor at a major university gave a lecture that advocated "curing homosexuality," there'd be an outcry and likely an administrative reprimand. If a researcher wrote an article framing homosexuality as a medical pathology and advocating for gay conversion therapy, and submitted it to a journal dedicated to queer studies or LGBTQ health, it would be sternly rejected. And yet, even universities that put on a public show of embracing neurodiversity are still willing to employ faculty who speak of autistic people in pathologizing terms and advocate subjecting autistic children to abusive conversion therapy techniques like Applied Behavior Analysis—and that same sort of bigotry is still blithely published by academic journals and academic publishing imprints.

This sort of thing will continue as long as we allow it to continue—and we don't have to allow it to continue. Overt homophobia and racism are becoming increasingly unacceptable and difficult to get away with in mainstream academic discourse these days, and that's a positive development which began with relatively small groups of people in academia deciding that they weren't going to silently accept that sort of thing anymore. Challenging oppressive discourses is an uphill battle at first, but I take heart when I look at how much the academic discourse on homosexuality has shifted during my own lifetime. We can do this.

The Story Behind "Neurotypical Psychotherapists & Autistic Clients"

Since 2010, I've been a faculty member at California Institute of Integral Studies, a school known for its excellent Counseling Psychotherapy graduate programs. Most of the grad students in my classes are in training to become psychotherapists, and many of the students in my undergraduate classes are also headed in that direction.

By 2014, largely as a result of the essays on my website getting shared and discussed on social media, interest in my work had expanded beyond the autistic community and I was getting requests for consultation from psychotherapists and other professionals. I occupied an unusual niche, as someone who was both autistic *and* knowledgeable in the ways of psychotherapy (there are more people sharing that niche with me these days then there were back then, but not as many as I hope to see eventually). Some of the professionals who contacted me encouraged me to write up some guidelines for working with autistic clients.

What finally helped me get around to writing such a thing was an email from Sarah Coenen and Helen Cha-Choe, a pair of Counseling Psychotherapy grad students at California Institute of Integral Studies. I'd never met them, but Sarah and Helen were taking a Research Methods course taught by my friend and colleague Eri Çela. As their final project for that class, they wanted to research the attitudes of neurotypical psychotherapists toward autistic clients, and how those attitudes affected the quality of their work with those clients. Eri pointed them in my direction. They went to my website and read "Throw Away the Master's Tools" and "Neurodiversity: Some Basic Terms & Definitions," then contacted me with some follow-up questions.

I was delighted to learn that their project was grounded in the neurodiversity paradigm. Sarah and Helen recognized that the capacity of non-autistic professionals to work well with autistic clients was a form of cultural competency, and that the pathology paradigm constituted an obstacle to such competency and engendered condescending and unempathic attitudes toward autistic clients. Their clear understanding of the topic, and their excellent questions, inspired me to answer them at length. Having done so, I realized I'd finally managed to write the sort of advice to professionals that folks had been asking me to write. So in December of 2014 I put my answers to Sarah and Helen's questions up on my website, and now I'm reprinting it here.

In my answer to the second question, there's a bit where I say "Listen to autistic people, and read what we write," and then I list a few essential readings. I've edited the online version a few times over the years to update the list of readings I recommend, because new stuff keeps coming along that's better than the old stuff. Unfortunately, I won't be able to do that with the list in this version of the piece, because, well, it's printed in a book. The small handful of readings I've recommended in this version are so good that I'm confident they'll remain relevant for a long time, but I'm also confident that more great material that I want to recommend to psychotherapists working with autistic clients will come along in the years after this book is published.

Neurotypical Psychotherapists & Autistic Clients

*Q: How would you address empathy deficits and poor communi-
cation skills in neurotypical people working with autistic clients?*

The 20th Century political scientist Karl Deutsch said, "Power is the
ability not to have to learn."

I quote this statement often, because I think it's one of the most
important truths ever articulated about privilege, oppression, and
social power relations.

When a social system is set up such that one particular group is
almost always in a position of social power or privilege over another group, the members of the privileged group never truly need to
learn or practice empathy or understanding for the members of the
disempowered, oppressed group. Nor do the members of the privileged group need to learn to adapt to the communication style of
the oppressed group.

Neurotypical privilege means that neurotypical people interacting with autistic people—particularly when the neurotypical people in question are in positions of professional authority—have the

luxury of never having to address or even acknowledge their own empathy deficits or poor communication skills, because they can blame all failures of empathy, understanding, and communication on the alleged deficits of the autistic people.

Anthropologist Mary Catherine Bateson, writing about learning and power relations in colonialism, observed that "People who don't wear shoes learn the languages of people who do, not vice versa."

Bateson's wording of this insight is especially resonant for the autistic community: when autistic activists object to the pathologization and abuse of autistic children by neurotypical parents and professionals, or the murder of autistic children by neurotypical parents, neurotypicals often attempt to silence us by condescendingly admonishing us to "put ourselves in the shoes" of the perpetrators. Yet as neurodiversity activist Kassiane Asasumasu has pointed out, not only do these same neurotypical parents and professionals never seriously attempt to put themselves in the shoes of autistic people, they do not even "acknowledge that we *have* shoes," metaphorically speaking.

Power—or privilege, as we now more commonly call the particular kind of power to which Deutsch was referring—is the ability not to have to learn. There's a phrase, "check your privilege," that's often repeated but is rarely understood or heeded by those privileged persons at whom it is directed. If we start from Deutsch's definition of power or privilege as the ability not to have to learn, we can understand "check your privilege" to mean, at least in part, "*Learn!* Be quiet, pay attention, and learn. *Learn,* even though the learning process, and the level of profound humility it requires, is going to be uncomfortable. Learn even though, because of your privilege, this sort of learning and humility is a discomfort that you have the luxury of being able to avoid—a luxury that we didn't have, when we had to learn your ways. Learn even though you don't have to."

Unfortunately, as members of all oppressed groups discover, most privileged people just won't do that. The states of profound mindfulness, humility, openness to correction, and tolerance for uncertainty that such learning demands are too far outside of most people's comfort zones. Most human beings simply won't go that far outside of their comfort zones if they don't have to. And privilege means they don't have to.

The system is currently set up so that when neurotypical professionals work with autistic individuals, the neurotypical professional is always in the role of greater authority: neurotypical therapist and autistic client; neurotypical doctor and autistic patient; neurotypical educator and autistic student; neurotypical researcher and autistic subject.

As long as this is the case, as long as neurotypical professionals only have regular, close contact with autistic individuals in situations that are set up such that the neurotypical professionals hold greater authority and power, the neurotypical professionals will never *have to* subject themselves to the uncomfortable humility of checking their privilege, will never *have to* learn real empathy and understanding for the autistic, and will never *have to* learn to understand and adapt to autistic forms of communication.

And if they don't have to, most of them won't.

A related consideration is that when a person's entire experience of an oppressed group consists of situations in which the members of that group are in "inferior" roles, it inevitably shapes that person's perspective on the group in question. Just look at the Stanford Prison Experiment, for a glimpse of how quickly and powerfully this effect kicks in.

Anyone who understands this phenomenon will be unsurprised to learn that in my experience, the people who have the *least* empathy for autistic persons, the *least* ability to communicate respectful-ly with autistic persons, and the *least* genuine openness to learning from autistic persons, are the neurotypical professionals who have spent their careers working with autistic persons, in situations in which the professional always holds the authority and the autistic persons are always in the role of the patient, student, research subject, or "recipient of services."

It's nearly impossible for professionals of that sort to make the shift to the neurodiversity paradigm, to learn to check their neu-rotypical privilege, or to start respectfully listening to and learning from autistic perspectives. They've simply become too entrenched in the habit of not seeing autistic persons as equals.

So my answer to the question of how to address empathy deficits and poor communication skills in neurotypical people working with autistic populations? Change the system, such that no neurotypical professional is permitted to work with autistic populations unless all of the following conditions are met:

1. The neurotypical professional must have received extensive training from autistic teachers, using curricula designed or approved by autistic experts. The autistic teachers and etx-perts in question must themselves be well-versed in the neu-rodiversity paradigm—and in realms of critical and libera-tory theory like Critical Psychology, Liberation Psychology, Disability Studies, Critical Autism Studies, and Queer Stud-ies—rather than tame, token autistic persons (like Temple Grandin) who have themselves internalized and accepted the language of the pathology paradigm and the ableism of the dominant culture.

2.   The neurotypical professional must be licensed to work with autistic populations, by a licensing board composed primarily of autistic persons well-versed in the neurodiversity paradigm.

3.   The work of the neurotypical professional must be subject to supervision, input, and audit by autistic representatives of the aforementioned licensing board, who have the authority to make recommendations to the board regarding the status of the neurotypical professional's license.

None of these suggestions are likely to be implemented in the society in which we currently live, of course. But it's a solution to the problems mentioned in your question—one of the only solutions to those problems that, if it were someday implemented, would actually work. And even when such solutions seem a long way off, one must dare to dream.

Q: What advice and or suggestions can you offer psychotherapists working with autistic clients?

Check your privilege.

Empty your cup, as the Zen Buddhists say.

Make the shift to the neurodiversity paradigm, completely. Throw out everything you've learned that's in any way based in the pathology paradigm, all the messages about autism that you've been fed by the dominant culture. Be ferociously, eternally diligent about this: sociocultural programming is a constantly ongoing process, so breaking your sociocultural programming must also be a constantly ongoing process, and you'll be swimming against the current. And it's harder for members of privileged groups than members of oppressed groups: the status quo works in your favor, makes you the authority, lets you stay in your comfort zone, so it requires enormous ongoing commitment to stay mindful of the insidious and pervasive influence of the dominant paradigm, and to go against it.

The master's tools will never dismantle the master's house, but throwing away the master's tools is hard—and it's ten times harder if, within the current status quo, you're one of the masters.

Recognize that nearly everything written or taught about neurodivergence by neurotypical "experts" is just plain wrong, and is harmful to your autistic clients. The dominant culture's stereotypes about any oppressed group are not more true just because you read them in a book or article written by an "expert." Remember that there has been plenty of work published in the past by "experts"— including psychologists—that promoted sexist and racist stereotypes under the guise of "science."

Remember that an author, teacher, researcher, or other "expert" who refers to autism, for instance, as a "disorder," is no more of a trustworthy, unbiased, "objective" authority than an "expert" who refers to homosexuality as a "disorder," or than the "experts" who used to describe non-white peoples as "savage."

Remember that if you use the language of the pathology paradigm, you are reinforcing a social paradigm that harms your clients, and thus you are working against your clients' interests.

Seek out autistic teachers, supervisors, and consultants who are well-versed in the neurodiversity paradigm. And pay them for their work. It's remarkable how many neurotypical professionals and organizations are happy to pay neurotypical "experts" to talk about autistic people, but balk at paying the same rates for the harder-earned expertise of actual autistic people.

Listen to autistic people, and read what we write. Read autistic scholars and activists like Remi Yergeau, Kassiane Asasumasu, Amy Sequenzia, and myself. Read Yergeau's book *Authoring Autism* and their article "Clinically Significant Disturbance." Read Finn V. Gratton's *Supporting Transgender Autistic Youth and Adults*. Read Michael Scott Monje's *Defiant*. Read neuroqueer speculative fiction by autistic authors like Dora M. Raymaker and Ada Hoffmann.

Never attempt to cure your client of being autistic. When you have an autistic client suffering from anxiety and depression, for instance, remember that your job is to treat the client for anxiety and depression, not for autism. Professionals who truly understand the neurodiversity paradigm would no sooner attempt to "treat" a client's autism than attempt to "treat" a client's homosexuality, or attempt to "treat" a client's ethnicity.

Familiarize yourself with the field of Liberation Psychology, and be continually aware that many of the psychological issues with which your autistic clients struggle will be issues created by social injustice and oppression, rather than by the client's innate qualities. And remember that a good treatment plan is likely to include helping a client recognize this fact—helping the client understand their own oppression, both external and internalized, as a primary cause of their suffering.

Indeed, remember that your client may have completely bought into the pathology paradigm and may be ignorant of and even resistant to the neurodiversity paradigm. In which case, in order to support your client's psychological well-being and liberation, it may be your duty as a therapist to introduce your client to the neurodiversity paradigm, and to educate your client by pointing them to writings like the ones mentioned above.

And above all, check your privilege.

Q: How does your training in somatics (both as a therapeutic orientation and your aikido background) factor into your work in the Neurodiversity Movement?

I see *cognitive liberty* as a core value of the Neurodiversity Movement.

The term *cognitive liberty* was coined by Wrye Sententia and Richard Glen Boire, the founders of the Center for Cognitive Liberty and Ethics. Cognitive liberty as an ethical value boils down to the idea that individuals have the right to absolute sovereignty over their own brains and their own cognitive processes. Advocates of cognitive liberty often break this idea down into two fundamental guiding ethical principles (originally inspired by the two "commandments" offered by Timothy Leary in *The Politics of Ecstasy*):

1. Individuals have the right to not have their brains and cognitive processes tampered with non-consensually.

2. Individuals have the right to tamper with their own brains and cognitive processes, or to voluntarily have them tampered with, in any way they choose.

Those of us who are deeply involved in transformative somatic practices or in the field of Somatic Psychology understand that the psyche is somatically organized, which means that each individual's distinctive neurocognitive processes are intimately entwined with that individual's style of movement and embodiment. Changes in movement and embodiment create changes in cognition.

This means that to tamper with a person's unique individual style of movement and embodiment (for instance, through the behaviorist techniques that are frequently used to make autistic children suppress the outward signs of autism) is to tamper with that person's cognition, and thus to violate their cognitive liberty.

In other words, freedom of embodiment—that is, the freedom to indulge, adopt, and/or experiment with any styles or quirks of movement and embodiment, whether they come naturally to one or whether one chooses them—is an essential element of cognitive liberty, and thus an essential area of focus for the Neurodiversity Movement. The freedom to be autistic necessarily includes the freedom to give bodily expression to one's neurodivergence.

For somatically-oriented psychotherapists, one important implication of all this is that autistic clients will often have acquired habitual unconscious tensions (what Wilhelm Reich referred to as *character armor*) that prevent them from giving full expression to the movement style that is natural and optimal for them. These tensions will tend to be especially severe and deep-rooted in clients who, in childhood, were frequently shamed or otherwise abused for their physical expressions of neurodivergence, or who were subjected to behaviorist "therapies" or other forms of coerced physical conformity.

An integration of the neurodiversity paradigm into the field of Somatic Psychology would include the recognition of these habitual tensions as somatic manifestations of internalized oppression. And it seems to me that somatically-oriented psychotherapists, once they have embraced the neurodiversity paradigm, are uniquely qualified to assist autistic clients in the task of liberating themselves from the bonds of such tensions, and thus recovering their capacity for giving full expression to their unique potentials.

Guiding Principles for a Course on Autism

In 2014, I was invited to create and teach a course called Critical Perspectives on Autism and Neurodiversity in the undergraduate Interdisciplinary Studies program at California Institute of Integral Studies. I taught that course a couple of times, and in 2016 I wrote this piece inspired by the experience. In 2018, I was invited to create and teach an updated version of the course for the school's new undergraduate Psychology program. As of this writing in 2021, that course has evolved into Introduction to Neurodiversity Studies, and is part of the undergraduate Psychology program's core curriculum. In fact, one of the reasons I'm writing this book now is so I can use it as one of the textbooks for the course.

I originally published this piece on my Neurocosmopolitanism website in July of 2016. It was the final essay that I wrote for that site, before turning my attention to other sorts of writing in other venues. The quality of thought and writing in this piece strikes me as a significant step up from my earlier essays.

It's got a distinctly neuroqueer vibe, at least to my eye, which might have something to do with the fact that I wrote it while I was just beginning to come to terms with being transgender. I think it makes for a good conclusion to this part of the book, and a good segue into the material that's more directly focused on neuroqueering.

"The classroom remains the most radical space of possibility in the academy." —bell hooks

Early on in the process of designing my *Critical Perspectives on Autism and Neurodiversity* course for the undergraduate program at California Institute of Integral Studies, I asked myself the question, "What are the most essential and indispensable guiding principles any course on autism must follow, in order to ensure that the course truly remains grounded in the neurodiversity paradigm and avoids inadvertently reinforcing the attitudes of the pathology paradigm on any level?" I eventually developed a list of seven such guiding principles, which have served me quite well and which are here enumerated in the hope that they will be useful to others in creating similar courses.

1. To Hell with "Balance"

A good course on autism (or, for that matter, a good piece of writing on autism, or good education or journalism on autism in any medium) should not attempt to strike any sort of "balance" between the neurodiversity paradigm and the pathology paradigm. The pathology paradigm is simply an outgrowth of cultural ableism and bigotry. Work based in the pathology paradigm has no more scholarly or "scientific" validity than work based in cultural paradigms of racism, misogyny, or homophobia. Like racism, misogyny, and homophobia, the pathology paradigm is just plain wrong. The fact that at this point in history nearly *all* mainstream academic and professional writing on autism is based in the pathology paradigm doesn't make it any less wrong. There was a time that nearly all mainstream academic and professional writing on race was racist, and that didn't make racism valid or right.

A good educator should seek to expose students to good information while steering them away from ignorance and bigotry. A "balance" between right and wrong isn't right; a "balance" between good information and ignorant bigotry isn't superior to good information. So, to hell with "balance." If you were teaching an African-American Studies course, would you insist that half of the assigned readings consist of racist literature by white supremacists, in the interest of "balance"? I certainly hope not.

Consider also that the pathology paradigm is so dominant and pervasive in academia and in society as a whole that all students in any course on autism have grown up thoroughly steeped in the assumptions of the pathology paradigm, and it's likely that nearly everything they've been taught about autism has been based in the pathology paradigm. Students come into a class on autism already heavily biased toward the pathology paradigm and with heads already full of the bigoted misconceptions about autism engendered by the pathology paradigm, and outside of the class they'll continue to dwell in a world in which the pathology paradigm is constantly reinforced. Thus, even if "balance" were our priority, courses that are entirely and intentionally weighted toward the neurodiversity paradigm are merely a small step toward *restoring* balance in a world that's overwhelmingly biased toward the pathology paradigm.

So a good course on autism should actively and uncompromisingly promote the neurodiversity paradigm, just as a good African-American Studies course is actively and uncompromisingly anti-racist. Work based in the pathology paradigm, if it's assigned at all, should be assigned only so that the instructor and students can critique it in order to hone the students' skills at recognizing and critiquing such work.

2. The Instructor Must Be Autistic

The instructor must be autistic. Imagine the outcry that would (rightly) ensue if a college's courses in Women's Studies were primarily taught by men, or if a college's courses on African-American Studies were primarily taught by white people! The fact that it's still widely regarded as acceptable for courses on autism to be mostly taught by non-autistic people is an indicator of just how deeply the pathology paradigm pervades the mindset of our society. Regardless of the curriculum, every course on autism that isn't taught by an autistic instructor implicitly reinforces the pathology paradigm and the ableist assumption that non-autistic persons are better qualified to speak for and about autistic persons than autistic persons themselves. There are enough out-of-the-closet autistics in academia these days that any college should be able to find one to teach a course on autism. And given how heavily most hiring processes discriminate against autistics, the autistic academics could certainly use the work.

3. The Instructor Must Be a Participant in Autistic Culture, Community, and Resistance

When academic institutions do invite an autistic person to have any sort of significant voice in their curriculum on autism, the autistic person in question is nearly always chosen from a short list of well-known autistics whom I have come to think of as the *tame autistics*. The tame autistics all have certain traits in common: they are white;

they are heterosexual, asexual, and/or fairly closeted about their sexuality; they grew up fairly affluent and have never faced extreme poverty or homelessness; they are highly capable of oral speech; they are ableist, and have no problem with pathologizing non-speaking autistics or other autistics who are significantly more disabled than themselves; they regard disability as shameful and tend to avoid describing themselves as disabled; they rarely contradict non-autistic "autism experts" or ableist autism organizations run by non-autistic people; they have few (if any) close autistic friends and have never been deeply involved in the radical activist autistic culture and communities from which the Neurodiversity Movement emerged; they have appropriated the term "neurodiversity" now that it's becoming a well-known buzzword, but their thinking remains rooted in the pathology paradigm. Temple Grandin and John Elder Robison are probably the best-known of these tame autistics at the time that I write this, but there are many others—in fact, there are a couple of publishing companies, specializing in autism-related books based in the pathology paradigm, that actively seek the work of tame autistic authors.

Autistic though they may be, none of these tame autistics would be equipped to create or teach a curriculum that poses real critical challenges to the pathology paradigm and to the bigotry of the dominant cultural narratives around autism. For a course to be effective in serving those goals, it's not enough for the instructor to be autistic; the instructor must be an autistic with a substantial history of active participation in autistic culture and community, including autistic rights activism, resistance to oppressive cultural and professional practices based in the pathology paradigm, and celebration of autistic pride.

4. Autistic Voices Must Be Central

The writings and perspectives of actual autistic persons must be central, not peripheral, to the curriculum. At least 80% of the assigned readings should be by autistic authors. Tame autistics don't count—not that the course can't include any material by tame autistics, but such material should be approached with the explicit intent of critiquing the internalized oppression of the authors, and the way that the work of such authors tends to perpetuate the pathologizing narratives that the authors have been taught to impose on their lives. A course in which most of the readings by autistics are by tame autistics is a course that reinforces dominant cultural narratives rather than challenging them.

5. Truth Is Where It Is

In the realm of conventional academic literature (e.g., peer-reviewed journals and books from mainstream academic presses) the discourse on autism is dominated by the voices of non-autistic writers whose work is based in the pathology paradigm. Autistic voices and narratives that pose critical challenges to this dominant discourse, and to the host of beliefs and practices around autism that are rooted in the pathology paradigm, are systematically marginalized in this literature—excluded, silenced, disingenuously misinterpreted, or condescendingly dismissed.

To find the autistic voices that challenge the assumptions and practices of the dominant paradigm through various combinations of personal testimony and direct critique, one must generally look outside the well-guarded walls of mainstream academic literature. Until quite recently, nearly all of the most important work by non-tame autistic authors could only be found on the internet. While autistic work based in the neurodiversity paradigm is now beginning to gain footholds in academia—particularly with the recent emergence of the fields of Neurodiversity Studies and Critical Autism Studies—the leading edges of liberatory autistic thought still tend to initially emerge online or through the efforts of independent publishing houses like Autonomous Press that specifically seek to amplify marginalized voices. Given this state of affairs, the list of assigned readings for a course on autism based in the neurodiversity paradigm rather than the pathology paradigm must necessarily consist to a significant degree of materials drawn from sources outside of the realm of conventional academic publishing.

The instructor ought to make a point of explaining all of this on the first day of class, and perhaps also articulate it in the syllabus. It's good for students to understand the rationale behind an unorthodox reading list; it's also good for students to understand how the gatekeeping systems of conventional academic literature resist incursions by marginalized voices that pose radical challenges to dominant paradigms—and how such challenges, as a result, tend to emerge outside the borders of mainstream academia and only gradually fight their way inward.

6. The Instructor Must Model the Accommodation of Neurodivergence

Most academic settings reflect the ableist and neuronormative values of the dominant culture. Students are expected to conform to the dominant neuronormative conventions of learning and participation, and students whose learning and access needs conflict with those conventions are heavily discriminated against in most educational institutions. The instructor must openly and explicitly declare the class a zone of freedom from this sort of discrimination and compulsory neuronormativity, and must clearly and consistently demonstrate the creative accommodation of neurodivergence and individual access needs in her conduct of the class.

An instructor may assign a superb list of readings on the neurodiversity paradigm, and may speak eloquently on the importance of embracing neurodiversity and accommodating the access needs of neurodivergent persons—but if the instructor does not model this embracing and accommodation of neurodivergence in how she actually conducts the class and deals with the students, then the instructor's hypocrisy will ultimately undermine her message and the course will be a hollow sham. One cannot convincingly challenge a paradigm of compulsory neuronormativity while remaining complicit in the institutionalized enforcement of that same neuronormativity. In the immortal words of Audre Lorde, the master's tools will never dismantle the master's house.

It is not sufficient for the instructor to only grant students the accommodations that are mandated for them by the college's Disability Services department. This is merely compliance with the law (although many instructors and many institutions resist even doing that much). Disability Services departments in the world of higher education reinforce the pathology paradigm by demanding that neurodivergent students subject themselves to the process of being professionally diagnosed, and of having their divergences from neuronormativity pathologized as "disorders," before accommodations are granted. Thus, any instructor who provides accommodations only when required by the Disability Services department is also implicitly reinforcing and condoning the pathology paradigm.

Instead, on the first day of class, the instructor should explicitly point out the above dynamics, and should invite all students to publicly or privately speak up about any access needs they have that they're aware of or that they might become aware of during the course of the term. The instructor should do her best to work with the students to accommodate their needs. If there are accommodations that neither the instructor nor the student can provide, and Disability Services and/or other institutional departments must be involved, then the instructor should advocate for the student with those departments if such advocacy can help to expedite the provision of the needed accommodations.

Conflicts between the access needs of different individuals should be negotiated in class as part of the learning process. For instance, I often get students who need to take notes on laptops, tablets, or other electronic devices, because they need the notes in order to retain information but they can't write quickly enough by hand. Personally, I can't focus on speaking and listening to the class while someone next to me is noisily tap-tap-tapping away at a keyboard. So, right at the beginning of the first day of class (when I'm teaching in person rather than online), I tell students that they're welcome to type during class as long as they don't sit too close to me—there's a "no typing zone" around the front of the room where I'm positioned, and a "typing zone" across the room from me. This works for everyone—and more importantly, it immediately provides students with an example of what access needs are and how they can be civilly negotiated.

7. The Instructor Must Model and Invite the Embodied Expression of Neurodivergence

In the classroom, students must be free to *be* neurodivergent, to *act* neurodivergent, to *look* and *sound* neurodivergent. Each student must be free to openly engage in whatever forms and styles of embodiment and movement come naturally to them, or meet their (physical, cognitive, and/or emotional) needs, or emerge as spontaneous responses to external or internal circumstances. The classroom must be declared a zone of freedom from the dominant culture's pervasive requirement that everyone strive to constantly perform neuronorma-tivity. Students must instead be invited to drop the performance of neuronormativity and to freely explore and indulge in the *embodied* performance of neurodivergence.

It is not sufficient for the instructor to merely tell students that in this class it's okay for them to give expression to their neurodiver-gence. Sociocultural pressures to perform neuronormativity are life-long, pervasive, and insidious. By the time people are old enough to end up in a college classroom, they have almost always internalized these pressures to the point where they habitually police themselves and engage in the performance of neuronormativity even in situ-ations in which it isn't explicitly required of them by any external authority. That's how enculturation works, and how internalized op-pression works on an embodied level. Internalized normativity is a powerful force, especially when engrained into habits of embodied performance.

Thus, in order for the classroom to actually function as any sort of zone of liberation from compulsory neuronormativity, it is necessary for the instructor to explain all of this—to explain how the domi-nant culture entrains us all toward the performance of normativity, and how this performance becomes internalized and habituated on a bodily level, and how breaking out of that shell of normative perfor-mance is an essential component of self-liberation. It is necessary for the instructor to explicitly declare the classroom a zone for free ex-perimentation with shedding habits of normative performance and actively exploring, practicing, reclaiming, and cultivating non-nor-mative modes of embodiment. And it is necessary for the instructor to personally practice what she preaches: to personally, physically model the embodied expression of neurodivergence. The autistic instructor must move like an autistic person, must freely and visibly follow her natural movement impulses in the classroom. Most students simply will not dare to engage in such exploration in the classroom unless the instructor leads the way. And this means, of course, that in order to be qualified to teach in a way that liberates others, the instructor must do the work of self-liberation on a bodily level.

Conducting the class in this manner is obviously both liberatory and educational (it's fascinating and edifying to observe the many different forms and styles of movement that gradually emerge in the classroom). What may be less obvious is that this is as much about access as about liberation. To whatever extent they think about access needs in the classroom at all, most people tend to think in terms of eliminating physical barriers (e.g., by providing wheelchair access, captioned videos, or lighting that doesn't trigger seizures), or accommodating atypical learning styles (e.g., by giving dyslexic students extra time on quizzes). Both of these, of course, are essential forms of accommodation. But freedom of embodiment is also an access need. A student who must constantly exert her energy and attention toward passing for "normal"—i.e., performing neuronormativity rather than allowing their natural neurodivergent styles of movement and embodiment to come to the surface—is a student who has less energy and attention available for the tasks of learning and creative participation. Students can be better students when they're given the space to move in the ways that are optimal for the functioning of their particular neurologies, rather than the ways that are required for the performance of normativity.

Here, again, conflicting access needs can be openly negotiated in class as part of the learning experience. If one student needs to drum her fingers on the desktop and another needs quiet, then perhaps the drummer can place a folded scarf or other article of clothing on the desktop to create a quieter drumming surface. If one student needs to stand up and make dance-like full-body movements, and others find this visually distracting, perhaps a corner of the room that's outside of the visual field of the seated students can become the designated dancing space.

Just as intentionally liberating oneself from the culturally in-grained and enforced performance of heteronormativity is sometimes referred to as *queering,* intentionally liberating oneself from the cul-turally ingrained and enforced performance of neuronormativity can be thought of as *neuroqueering.* To invite the embodied expression of neurodivergence in the classroom is a way of neuroqueering the classroom space, and an invitation to students to engage in the prac-tice of neuroqueering. The concept of neuroqueering represents a rich and important intersection of the fields of Neurodiversity Stud-ies and Queer Theory, and, on top of its other benefits, introducing the practice of neuroqueering embodiment into the classroom is an excellent way to introduce neuroqueering as a concept.

In Conclusion

The present state of autism-related discourse, theory, and praxis in the academic and professional spheres is deplorable. The discourse and theory reflect a level of ignorance and bigotry that would be regarded as scandalous in most academic circles today if it involved any other historically oppressed group. The praxis generated by this shoddy discourse and theory consistently makes life worse for autis-tic persons and their families; the situation is so bad that harm, deg-radation, and trauma suffered at the hands of therapists, educators, and other professionals has become one of the most consistent and pervasive themes in the writings of autistics. This whole sorry state of affairs can be traced directly to the dominance of the pathology paradigm, which assumes as a starting premise that autistic minds and lives are intrinsically defective and inferior. There is simply no way to generate good theory and praxis by clinging to unsound and bigoted assumptions.

Substantial change for the better will only come from abandoning the pathology paradigm and making the shift to the neurodiversity paradigm. For such a shift to happen, the next generation of professionals must be educated on autism from a perspective based solidly in the neurodiversity paradigm, and must be inoculated against the pathology paradigm by being trained to recognize and critique it as a manifestation of cultural prejudice possessing no more scientific validity than any other form of bigotry.

The seven principles I've delineated are intended to serve as a foundational set of guidelines for creating college courses that provide this sort of critical education on autism. It is my hope that sharing these ideas will encourage the creation of many other courses in other schools, built upon similar principles and with the same intent to prepare new generations of students to be active participants in creating the much-needed shift from the pathology paradigm to the neurodiversity paradigm in the academic and professional discourse on autism.

PART III:
POSTNORMAL POSSIBILITIES

*"'Queer,' in any case, does not designate a class
of already objectified pathologies or perversions;
rather, it describes a horizon of possibility whose
precise extent and heterogeneous scope cannot in
principle be delimited in advance."*

David M. Halperin

Neuroqueer: An Introduction

I originally wrote this piece and published it on my website on May 2, 2015. As the concept of neuroqueer(ing) has caught on and sparked imaginations, it's become one of my more frequently cited writings.

I coined the term *neuroqueer* in a paper I wrote for a grad school class in the Spring of 2008. Over the next several years, I played with it in further grad school papers, in private conversations, and in the ongoing development of my own thoughts and practices. The concept of neuroqueer, or of *neuroqueering* (I've always seen it as a verb first and an adjective second), increasingly came to inform my thinking, my embodiment, and my approach to life.

When I first started publishing pieces of my writing on neurodiversity in 2012, I wasn't ready to put the term neuroqueer out into the world yet. I wanted more time to let it simmer, to think and feel my way into its nuances and implications. In early 2014, though, I mentioned it in in a small private Facebook group for autistic bloggers, and discovered that my friend and colleague Athena Lynn Michaels-Dillon had also come up with the term independently and had also been playing around with it, letting it simmer, and thinking about putting it into publication eventually. Another dear friend and colleague, Remi Yergeau, who was also in that discussion, revealed that although the term neuroqueer was new for them, they'd been thinking along quite similar and compatible lines in playing with the concept of "neurological queerness."

The three of us—Athena, Remi, and I—emerged from that conversation freshly inspired to begin introducing the term, and the set of concepts and practices it describes, into our public work and into our communities and the broader culture. Athena and I, along with our friend B. Martin Allen and others, founded the independent worker-owned publishing house Autonomous Press, and its imprint NeuroQueer Books, to publish books with neuroqueer themes (including the annual *Spoon Knife* multi-genre neuroqueer lit anthology).

Meanwhile, a couple of other members of that little Facebook group, who were involved in the discussion where Athena and Remi and I first discovered we'd each been playing with the same concept, became so excited about this new term that they immediately ran out and started spreading it around on various social media platforms. The word caught on like wildfire, much faster than its creators had imagined and much faster than we could keep up with. Soon it was showing up not only all over queer and neurodivergent social media spaces, but also in academic papers and conference presentations by people we'd never heard of.

(The day before I wrote this piece, I was at California Institute of Integral Studies teaching a new course on neurodiversity. I was introducing my students to basic neurodiversity-related terminology like *neurotypical* and *neurodivergent,* when a young undergraduate excitedly asked me, "Have you ever heard of the term *neuroqueer?*")

It was nice to see it catch on like that. There's a special kind of joy in bringing something new into the world and seeing it become meaningful to a lot of other people whom one hasn't even met. On the downside, the word was almost instantly appropriated by people whose understanding of it was far more narrow and simplistic than its creators had intended. I've seen a lot of interpretations of neuro-queer and attempts at definition from folks who've adopted the term, and sometimes those interpretations miss the point in ways that are truly facepalm-worthy. Other interpretations are a bit more on-point but overly narrow, and I find myself responding with, "Yeah, well, I suppose that's *part* of what we were getting at…"

So what *were* we getting at? What *is* neuroqueer (or neuroqueer-ness, or neuroqueering)?

I should first of all acknowledge that any effort to establish an "authoritative" definition of neuroqueer is in some sense inherent-ly doomed and ridiculous, simply because the sort of people who identify as neuroqueer and engage in neuroqueering tend to be the sort of people who delight in subverting definitions, concepts, and authority.

That said, the eight-point definition that follows is the closest thing to an "authoritative" (or at least creator-authorized) definition as is ever likely to exist. I wrote it with the input and approval of the other originators of the concept—so it's the one definition out there that all of the originators have agreed is not only accurate, but also inclusive of *all* of the various practices and ways-of-being that any of the three of us intended the word to encompass.

I originally conceived of *neuroqueer* as a verb: neuroqueering as the practice of queering (subverting, defying, disrupting, liberating oneself from) neuronormativity and heteronormativity simulta-neously. It was an extension of the way *queer* is used as a verb in Queer Theory; I was expanding the Queer Theory conceptualization of queering to encompass the queering of neurocognitive norms as well as gender norms—and, in the process, I was examining how socially-imposed neuronormativity and socially-imposed heteronormativity were entwined with one another, and how the queering of either of those two forms of normativity entwined with and blended into the queering of the other one.

So *neuroqueer* was a verb first, and then, like its root word *queer*, it was also an adjective. Even in that first paper in which I used the term in 2008, I used it as both a verb and an adjective. As a verb, it refers to a broad range of interrelated practices. As an adjective, it describes things that are associated with those practices or that result from those practices: neuroqueer theory, neuroqueer perspectives, neuroqueer embodiments, neuroqueer narratives, neuroqueer literature, neuroqueer art, neuroqueer culture, neuroqueer spaces.

And, just like *queer*, the adjective form of *neuroqueer* can also serve as a label of social identity. One can neuroqueer, and one can *be* neuroqueer. A neuroqueer individual is any individual whose identity, selfhood, gender performance, and/or neurocognitive style have in some way been shaped by their engagement in practices of neuroqueering, *regardless of what gender, sexual orientation, or style of neurocognitive functioning they may have been born with.*

Or, to put it more concisely (but perhaps more confusingly): you're neuroqueer if you neuroqueer.

So what does it mean to neuroqueer, as a verb? What are the various practices that fall within the definition of *neuroqueering?*

1. Being both neurodivergent and queer, with some degree of conscious awareness and/or active exploration around how these two aspects of one's being entwine and interact (or are, perhaps, mutually constitutive and inseparable).

2. Embodying and expressing one's neurodivergence in ways that also queer one's performance of gender, sexuality, ethnicity, and/or other aspects of one's identity.

3. Engaging in practices intended to undo and subvert one's own cultural conditioning and one's ingrained habits of neuronormative and heteronormative performance, with the aim of reclaiming one's capacity to give more full expression to one's uniquely weird potentials and inclinations.

4. Engaging in the queering of one's own neurocognitive processes (and one's outward embodiment and expression of those processes) by intentionally altering them in ways that create significant and lasting increase in one's divergence from prevailing cultural standards of neuronormativity and heteronormativity.

5. Approaching, embodying, and/or experiencing one's neurodivergence as a form of queerness (e.g., in ways that are inspired by, or similar to, the ways in which queerness is understood and approached in Queer Theory, Gender Studies, and/or queer activism).

6. Producing literature, art, scholarship, and/or other cultural artifacts that foreground neuroqueer experiences, perspectives, and voices.

7. Producing critical responses to literature and/or other cultural artifacts, focusing on intentional or unintentional characterizations of neuroqueerness and how those charac-

terizations illuminate and/or are illuminated by actual neuroqueer lives and experiences.

8. Working to transform social and cultural environments in order to create spaces and communities—and ultimately a society—in which engagement in any or all of the above practices is permitted, accepted, supported, and encouraged.

So there you have it, from the people who brought you the term. This definition is, again, not an authoritative "last word" on the subject, because that would be a silly thing to attempt. Rather, I hope this will be taken as a "first word"—a broad "working definition" from which further theory, practice, and play will proceed.

Happy neuroqueering!

Comments on "Neuroqueer: An Introduction"

Around the same time "Neuroqueer: An Introduction" appeared on my *Neurocosmopolitanism* website, Autonomous Press published the first edition of Athena Lynn Michaels-Dillon's semi-autobiographical neuroqueer novella *Defiant* (written under the pen name Michael Scott Monje). The word *neuroqueer* didn't appear in the text of *Defiant*, but its appearance on the back cover marked the word's first time in print.

Remi Yergeau, who at the time of our first discussion of neuroqueer(ing) had been playing around with the concept of autism as "neurological queerness" in the book they were working on, integrated the term *neuroqueer* into their manuscript, citing and quoting "Neuroqueer: An Introduction." Remi's book was published by Duke University Press in 2018 under the title *Authoring Autism: On Rhetoric and Neurological Queerness*; as of this writing, it remains the single best and most comprehensive critique of the rhetoric of the pathology paradigm and how the pathology paradigm informs (or rather, deforms) the discourse on autism and autistics.

My own work has been focused primarily on two aspects of neuroqueer(ing). The first aspect is neuroqueering as embodied practice—playing with the synthesis of the neurodiversity paradigm, queer theory, the field of somatic psychology, and transformative movement practices like aikido and physical theater. Neuroqueering as somatic praxis has been central to my conception of neuroqueer from the start. The 2008 grad school paper in which I first coined the term neuroqueer was written for the magnificent Dr. Ian J. Grand's magnificent Psychodynamics course in the Somatic Psychology program at California Institute of Integral Studies. Ian Grand shuffled off this mortal coil in 2017, and as of 2021 I'm teaching that same Psychodynamics course myself—doing my best to make the classroom a queerly creative space, or perhaps a creatively queer space, just like Ian made his classroom the sort of creative space into which a concept like neuroqueer could be born.

The second aspect of neuroqueer(ing) on which I've been focused is the fostering of neuroqueer literature. In my role as Managing Editor at Autonomous Press, especially through my involvement in our annual *Spoon Knife* literary anthology, I've done my best to contribute in any way I can to the development of an explicitly neuroqueer literature, particularly what I see as an emerging genre of neuroqueer speculative fiction.

•

The use of the adjective *neuroqueer* as a label of social identity, like *gay* or *trans* or *Asian-American*, wasn't part of my original conception of the word back in 2008. My background in transformative practices like aikido and zazen inclines me to focus more on practice than on fixed identity categories, and defining the sort of work I wanted to do was far more interesting to me than defining myself.

Six years later, though, as I discussed neuroqueer(ing) with Athena Lynn Michaels-Dillon and Remi Yergeau for the first time, we recognized that if we put this word out into the world and it caught on, some folks probably were going to adopt it as an identity label. We were okay with that possibility. We figured that if identifying as neuroqueer helped anyone to understand and define themselves—or, better still, to transform and create themselves—in a way that was liberating and empowering for them, then yay, we were all for it.

And that is, in fact, what's been happening. While a growing number of people use neuroqueer as the dual-purpose verb/adjective I originally intended it to be, many have also found it meaningful and empowering as a term of identity. I hear from them sometimes, or meet them, or see them talk about it online. It's made a positive difference for some folks to be able to describe themselves as neuro-queer, and this makes me happy just like it makes me happy when someone tells me that their lives have been changed for the better by my teaching or my writing. I'm glad to have offered something that makes a difference to someone.

What doesn't make me so happy, though, is that some of the people who've adopted neuroqueer as a term of identity have also tried to re-define the term in a narrow and exclusionary way, and have appointed themselves the arbiters of who gets call themselves neuroqueer.

So, let me make this clear: the essay "Neuroqueer: An Introduction" contains an intentionally broad list of practices that fall within the definition of neuroqueering. *Anyone* who engages in *any* of those practices can call themselves neuroqueer anytime they damn well want to. Anyone who says otherwise is misappropriating a concept intended to be liberatory, and turning it into just another excuse to form a special little club that they can exclude other people from to make themselves feel more important. Anyone trying to police other people's self-identities is just another tedious cop, and a cop is pretty much the most un-queer, non-liberatory thing a person can be.

It doesn't matter whether a person was born autistic, or born neurodivergent in any way. It doesn't matter what their gender or sexual orientation is. If they engage in neuroqueering, and they want to call themselves neuroqueer, they're welcome to, and it's no one else's business. A person who starts out neurotypical and heterosexual and cisgender, and chooses to intentionally engage in neuroqueering by creatively altering their own consciousness in ways that simultaneously queer their gender performance, has just as valid a claim to considering themselves neuroqueer as someone who was born autistic and gay.

If you see anyone trying to narrow the definition of neuroqueer and trying to police who gets to use the term, feel free to tell them that I said to stop acting like a fucking cop. The world needs more queering and fewer cops.

A Horizon of Possibility: Some Notes on Neuroqueer Theory

I'm typing these words on a cool foggy morning in Berkeley, California, in the Summer of 2021, and trying to wrap my brain around the fact that it's been fifteen years since I coined the term *neuroqueer*, seven years since the term leaked out into the sphere of public discourse via social media and began catching on considerably faster than I'd expected, and six years since I first published a brief working definition in the essay "Neuroqueer: An Introduction."

The concept of neuroqueer was born shortly after my daughter, and like my daughter it has a life of its own now and gets involved in all sorts of mischief that I don't find out about until well after it's happened. A lot of folks—most of whom I've never had any direct personal contact with—have adopted the term, used it in all manner of interesting ways in a variety of interesting contexts, and explored various aspects of its implications and potentials. I think this is fabulous.

For my own part, while my life and work have been increasingly informed by neuroqueer principles and practices—and while I've been closely involved in the emerging field of neuroqueer speculative fiction as both an author and an editor—apart from that little "Neuroqueer: An Introduction" essay I somehow haven't gotten around to writing up and publishing anything substantial about my own take on the meaning of neuroqueer or about the vistas of theory, praxis, and possibility toward which I've always intended the term to point. So this is where I finally get around to it.

The conceptualization of Neuroqueer Theory I'm presenting here is essentially the same as what I had in mind when I first came up with the term *neuroqueer* in 2008—though after a decade and a half of putting the theory into practice, and of refining both my ideas and my dubious writing skills, I can now articulate these concepts somewhat more clearly than I ever managed to do in my original awkward (and thankfully unpublished) grad school papers.

Four Realizations

The majority of people grow up believing their culture's socially-constructed gender norms to be "natural," and believing their socially-assigned gender roles and acquired habits of heteronormative gender performance to be innate and predetermined by biology. Queer Theory offers a different perspective, a perspective which recognizes the myriad ways in which the prevailing culture and its institutions work continually to impose heteronormative gender roles on each and every person, and to ingrain and enforce the performance of these roles—and a perspective which recognizes, also, that it is the sheer pervasiveness of this ongoing process which creates the compelling illusion that heteronormative gender roles are innate and natural. (Note that gender, as I'm using the term here, includes sexuality and sexual orientation, since heteronormative sexual behavior is part of the culturally-mandated performance of heteronormative gender roles.)

A central concept in Queer Theory, perhaps best articulated by Judith Butler in *Gender Trouble,* is that one's gender is constituted by one's ongoing performance of culturally conditioned habits of embodiment and activity. One's gender, in other words, is first and foremost something that one *does*—and therein lies the possibility of liberation from the confines of normativity. If gender is maintained through the habitual performance of specific actions, then heteronormativity and heteronormative gender roles can be subverted, transformed, modified, loosened, escaped from, and/or rendered more fluid, through engagement in practices that creatively deviate from and fuck with heteronormative performance. To engage in such practices is commonly referred to as *queering.*

The concept of *neuroqueering* came to me in 2008 when I was a grad student majoring in somatic psychology, a field which among other things studies how the organization and functioning of the psyche are entwined with the organization and usage of the body. I was writing a paper about how it harms autistic people to suppress their distinctively autistic modes of movement and embodiment in the interest of passing for neurotypical. Since the degree program I was in encouraged introspection and self-awareness, the paper included discussion of my own experience of masking my autistic modes of embodiment in order to survive my brutal childhood and young adulthood—and my subsequent process of learning to unmask and recover those autistic modes of embodiment (a project I was only just beginning to explore at that time, which eventually proved to be life-changing and which is still ongoing). As I worked on the paper, four realizations struck me in rapid succession:

1. The process of suppressing my visible expressions of autistic embodiment and trying to pass for neurotypical for the sake

of survival in my younger years seemed remarkably similar to the process of suppressing my femininity and trying to pass as a cisgender heterosexual male for the sake of survival in my younger years.

2.   If the process of liberating myself from my acquired habits of masculine gender performance and letting myself embody more fluid and feminine gender expressions could be described as a process of *queering heteronormativity*, then perhaps the process of liberating myself from my acquired habits of neurotypical performance and letting myself embody my neurodivergence could be described as *queering neuronormativity*.

3.   The more I reflected on the process by which I was pushed into the ill-fitting confines of heteronormative gender performance and the process by which I was pushed into the ill-fitting confines of neuronormative performance, the more it became clear that the two processes weren't merely similar or parallel: they were deeply and thoroughly entwined with one another, with no solid dividing line between them. Ultimately it wasn't two similar and parallel processes I was looking at, but a single multifaceted process.

4.   If the social imposition of heteronormative performance was inseparably entwined with the social imposition of neuronormative performance, then the process of liberating myself from the confines of heteronormative performance was also inseparably entwined with the process of liberating myself from neuronormative performance. The queering of

heteronormativity and the queering of neuronormativity were interconnected at some fundamental level. I couldn't truly liberate myself from heteronormativity without also liberating myself from neuronormativity, and I couldn't truly liberate myself from neuronormativity without also liberating myself from heteronormativity.

As I contemplated these realizations, the word *neuroqueer* suggested itself to me almost instantly. I incorporated the word into that paper I was working on, and ever since then I've been exploring its potentials as a foundation for creative theory-building and practice.

Beyond Neuroessentialism

The majority of thinkers within the neurodiversity movement and the emerging field of Neurodiversity Studies have thus far tended to view human neurodiversity through an essentialist lens in which each individual is seen as being neurotypical because they were born neurotypical, or neurodivergent because they were born neurodivergent (or because they became neurodivergent due to some event such as trauma or illness that significantly altered their neurocognitive functioning). This essentialist understanding of neurodiversity, which we might describe as *neuroessentialism*, has admittedly been useful in some respects. Much of the important work of the neurodiversity movement up to the present day has proceeded from the recognition that a great many people are indeed born neurodivergent—meaning that their bodyminds are predisposed to modes of functioning that are incompatible with neuronormative performance—and that attempting to force these people to comply with the standards of neuronormative performance is harmful, unethical, and oppressive. Without this understanding, a neurodiversity movement probably wouldn't have come into existence.

A neuroessentialist lens, however, also tends to impose artificial limitations on our sense of possibility. Here, again, we find parallels and connections between the realm of gender diversity and the realm of neurodiversity. The gender essentialist mindset, which can admit no gender possibilities other than two allegedly innate and immutable "biological sexes," is inimical to gender creativity and to the realization of the infinite range of gender possibilities. By the same token, an overly neuroessentialist mindset—a mindset which conceives of human neurodiversity as consisting of little more than an assortment of largely innate and immutable "neurotypes" or "types of brains"—is an obstacle to the realization of the infinite range of neurocognitive possibilities, and to the realization of our full potentials for intentional creative queering of our minds.

I'm not saying that it's not potentially useful for people to recognize themselves as autistic or dyslexic or whatever. When not pathologized or stigmatized, such categories can serve a variety of important purposes—including helping people to better understand themselves, to understand and communicate about their access needs and their experiences, and to connect with and work in solidarity with others who have similar neurocognitive tendencies and needs. What I'm saying here is that we shouldn't allow our conception of neurodiversity and its potentials to be constrained by such categories, just as we shouldn't allow our conceptions of gender and sexuality to be constrained by the binaristic categories of male and female, or gay and straight.

Public discourses on human diversity, including the discourses on gender, sexual orientation, and neurodiversity, occur almost entirely within the framework of identity politics—a framework which is fundamentally essentialist, since it involves sorting people into identity categories which tend to be presented as largely innate and immutable. Those who are accustomed to viewing queerness through this lens are often surprised to learn that the field of Queer Theory tends to reject essentialism and thus to depart radically from the premises of identity politics.

In conceptualizing gender as being constructed through ongoing socially instilled performances which can be subverted and altered (i.e., queered), Queer Theory frames identity as a fluid byproduct of activity: gender and sexuality are first and foremost things that one *does*, rather than things that one *is*, and *queer* is a verb first and an adjective second. In other words, one is queer not because one was born immutably queer on some sort of essential genetic level, but because one acts in ways which queer heteronormativity (e.g., going outside the boundaries of the binary gender category to which one was assigned at birth, or engaging in non-heteronormative sexual activity).

This is the case with Neuroqueer Theory as well. While *neurodivergent* is a category of identity, *neuroqueer* is first and foremost a verb. Neuroqueering is a practice, or, more accurately, a continually emergent and potentially infinite array of practices—modes of creatively subversive and transformative action in which anyone can choose to engage.

Of course, neuroqueer, like queer, can also function as an identity label. But while a person can be considered neurodivergent simply by virtue of having been born that way, what makes a person neuroqueer is their choice to engage in neuroqueering. One is neuroqueer not because one was born immutably neuroqueer, but because one acts in ways which queer neuronormativity (and remember that a core principle of Neuroqueer Theory is that neuronormativity and heteronormativity are fundamentally entwined with one another, and therefore any significant queering of neuronormativity is also inevitably a queering of heteronormativity).

Thus, Neuroqueer Theory applies the framework of Queer Theory to the realm of neurodiversity, and expands the scope of Queer Theory to encompass gender, sexuality, *and* neurodiversity, as well as the intersections of gender and sexuality *with* neurodiversity. As an extension of Queer Theory, Neuroqueer Theory is an approach to neurodiversity that radically departs from essentialist identity politics and seeks to transcend the constraints of neuroessentialism.

My favorite articulation of Queer Theory's transcendence of the limitations of essentialist identity politics is a single sentence penned in 1997 by queer theorist David M. Halperin. In his book *Saint Foucault: Towards a Gay Hagiography*, Halperin wrote:

"Queer," in any case, does not designate a class of already objectified pathologies or perversions; rather, it describes a horizon of possibility whose precise extent and heterogeneous scope cannot in principle be delimited in advance.

This post-essentialist articulation of the meaning and potentials of *queer* also perfectly sums up my conception of the meaning and potentials of *neuroqueer*. Neuroqueer is not a mere synonym for neurodivergent, or for neurodivergent identity combined with queer identity. Neuroqueer is active subversion of both neuronormativity and heteronormativity. Neuroqueer is intentional noncompliance with the demands of normative performance. Neuroqueer is choosing to actively engage with one's potentials for neurodivergence and queerness, and the intersections and synergies of those potentials. Neuroqueer is about recognizing the fundamentally entwined nature of cognition, gender, and embodiment, and also about treating cognition, gender, and embodiment as fluid and customizable, and as canvases for ongoing creative experimentation.

Neuroqueer transcends essentialist identity politics not only by treating identity as fluid and customizable, but also by being radically inclusive. Neuroqueering is something *anyone* can potentially do, and there are infinite possible ways to do it and infinite possible ways to be transformed by it. The term *neuroqueer* points to a horizon of creative possibility with which anyone can choose to engage.

I want to make it clear that I'm not in any way opposed to the use of the term *neuroqueer* as an identity label. Because I regard identity as fluid and customizable, and because I regard life as an ongoing process of self-creation, I'm in favor of people freely adopting any identity labels which might be meaningful to them. If identifying as neuroqueer serves in any way to improve your life or aid in your process of creative self-transformation, or even if it just appeals to you aesthetically, then go for it!

The reason I emphasize that neuroqueer is first and foremost a verb, and the reason I focus on neuroqueering as an emergent array of subversive and transformative practices, is that my central priority is the cultivation of human potentials for creativity, well-being, and beautiful weirdness—and our capacity to bring such potentials to realization ultimately depends not on our choice of identity labels but on our choice of practices. But of course, the strategic adoption of a new identity or name or label can itself function as a transformative practice.

Performance & Predisposition

While Neuroqueer Theory aims to transcend the limitations of essentialist identity politics, I also believe that the *complete* rejection of essentialism is a mistake which throws out the baby with the bathwater. Some prominent thinkers in the field of Queer Theory *do* reject essentialism completely, taking the position that gender is 100 percent socially constructed and socially instilled. My own position, which informs my conception of Neuroqueer Theory, is that both the essentialist and social constructionist models are overly reductionist when taken entirely on their own. I prefer a more complex hybrid understanding which incorporates elements of both models, and which probably boils down to something like 80 percent social constructionist and 20 percent essentialist. This hybrid understanding is based in the premise that although gender roles and the rules of gender performance are socially constructed and instilled, each individual human does also have their own unique set of more-or-less-innate tendencies and potentials (tendencies and potentials which have nothing whatsoever to do with the shape of a person's genitals or with so-called "biological sex").

The gender essentialist belief that heteronormative gender roles are innate and "natural" is patently absurd. First of all, the prevailing norms of gender role performance vary considerably from culture to culture, place to place, and historical period to historical period, with nearly every culture regarding its own current local norms as the one "natural" way to do gender. And second, if these norms were innate and "natural," cultures wouldn't have to put nearly so much effort into instilling and enforcing them.

On the other hand, the idea that a person's gender is *entirely* instilled by the external social world, with innate qualities and proclivities playing no part whatsoever in the shaping of an individual's experience and performance of gender, also seems rather implausible. Given the sheer intensity and pervasiveness of the heteronormative gender conditioning to which all of us are subjected from birth, surely few people would grow up to be gay or transgender if they didn't have some manner of internal disposition that was strong enough to make itself manifest even against the relentless tide of external social pressures.

Anyone who's spent time with babies knows that each one has their own distinct personality from birth. Not a fully-formed personality by any means, but at least an individual style comprised of a unique collection of personal inclinations. These innate inclinations, further shaped and developed through the infant's interactions with the physical/sensory world, constitute the inner foundation that child psychology pioneer D.W. Winnicott referred to as the *True Self*. Protean, malleable, and readily shaped by the external world as the young developing bodymind is, the distinctive tendencies, inclinations, and potentials of this core True Self nonetheless exert a significant influence on each individual's unique development—including a significant influence on how the social inculcation of gender roles is received, integrated, and expressed by that particular individual.

Consider the binary heteronormative masculine and feminine gender role performances that are commonly inculcated by the dominant cultures in the modern world. These gender role performances involve an extensive set of specific norms of embodiment (e.g., distinctive ways of walking, standing, sitting, moving, gesturing, speaking, dressing, engaging with and expressing emotions, doing sex and sexuality, physically interacting with the world and with others). None of these norms are genetically predestined or neurobiologically "hard-wired"; they're all culturally determined and socially instilled. The individual tendencies and inclinations that constitute the Winnicottian True Self, however, not only contribute at least some measure of unique style to a person's performance of the norms of their socially assigned and instilled gender role, but also determine how good a fit the assigned gender role and its norms are going to be for that particular person.

What I'm suggesting here is that although no one is *born* a straight cisgender heteronormative girl or woman, boy or man, some people are born with a collection of inner tendencies and potentials that are at least somewhat compatible with their local culture's norms of heterosexual feminine or masculine gender performance—thus enabling them to readily internalize those gender norms, to live within the parameters of those norms, and to come to experience their own socially instilled normative gender performance as "natural." When we describe someone as *cisgender*, we're referring to this condition of relative compatibility between the True Self and the social performance demands associated with their assigned gender.

At the other end of the spectrum, we find people in whom the tendencies and inclinations of the True Self are thoroughly incompatible with the norms governing the performance of the gender they were assigned at birth—incompatible to the point where performing their assigned gender causes them serious distress. For some of these people, the ones we refer to as *transgender*, the socially-constructed binary gender that they *weren't* assigned at birth (the so-called "opposite" gender) turns out to be a far better fit than the gender they were initially assigned. For others, neither of the binary gender options offered by the dominant heteronormative culture are a suitable fit.

Of course, all of this is somewhat of an oversimplification for the sake of brevity; it's entirely possible to be both transgender *and* nonbinary, for instance, and not all cultures limit themselves to a strict masculine/feminine binary when it comes to societally-approved gender options. The key point I'm making here is that while no one is born biologically predestined to "naturally" perform a specific gender in accordance with the gender norms of their native society, each individual does have their own particular predispositions which may make the socially-demanded heteronormative performance of their assigned gender viable and relatively intuitive for them, or somewhat less of a good fit, or highly uncomfortable, or downright impossible.

In this regard as in so many other regards, the dynamics of neuronormativity mirror and are entwined with the dynamics of heteronormativity. Like heteronormativity, neuronormativity is deeply ingrained in the prevailing culture and in all manner of social conventions, systems, and institutions. Like heteronormativity, neuronormativity is a pervasive social force, comprising a collection of innumerable culturally-constructed norms—norms related to nearly every aspect of embodiment, development, cognition, expression, communication, comportment, conduct, and interaction—which are socially modeled, inculcated, and enforced from birth onward in countless ways. And like heteronormativity, neuronormativity is to a large extent a matter of the ongoing habitual *performance* of internalized social norms.

Like heteronormative performance, neuronormative performance is a better fit for some folks than for others. At one end of the spectrum are those whose innate tendencies and inclinations are compatible enough with their local culture's standards of neuronormative performance that they readily internalize those standards and come to experience their own socially instilled performance of neuronormativity as "natural." This deep internalization and embodiment of the performance demands of neuronormativity, made possible when there is at least some basic degree of compatibility between those performance demands and the individual's innate capacities, is what we're really talking about when we refer to someone as neurotypical.

At the opposite end of the spectrum are those for whom the performance of neuronormativity is literally impossible—those who are absolutely unable to perform the actions necessary to maintain a neuronormative façade, and unable to suppress visibly non-neuronormative embodiments. In between the neurotypicals and those for whom neuronormative performance is an impossibility are those for whom neuronormativity is to some substantial degree incompatible with their natural tendencies and inclinations, such that neuronormative performance is a bad fit for them, is only partially possible and/or only sometimes possible for them, costs them significant effort, and is ultimately harmful for them to attempt to sustain.

Those who view neurodiversity through a neuroessentialist lens have an unfortunate tendency to compare and contrast neurotypicality with innate forms of neurodivergence like autism in a way that implicitly assumes autism and neurotypicality to be equally innate and equally intrinsic to a person's being. In the less well-informed discourses on neurodiversity that unfold on social media, for instance, one too often sees people speaking of "the neurotypical brain," as if neurotypicality were a biological destiny that unfolded inevitably from being born with a specific kind of brain.

On a strictly neurobiological level, there's not actually such a thing as a "normal brain" or a "neurotypical brain," any more than there's such a thing as a "male brain," a "heterosexual brain," or an "American brain." Neurotypical people aren't people who all share one distinct type of human brain, they're people whose compliance with prevailing cultural standards of neuronormative performance gains them the privileges that come with being considered "normal" within the dominant culture. Neurotypicality is more a social phenomenon than a biological one.

As previously noted, some people have more innate capacity than others to adapt to the demands of neuronormative performance. But having that capacity isn't the same as being innately neurotypical. If we begin from the premise that neurotypicality is performative in the same sense that heteronormative gender roles are performative, then a newborn infant can't be legitimately considered neurotypical for the same reason a newborn infant can't be legitimately considered a straight cisgender female or a straight cisgender male: newborn infants are obviously not engaged in enacting acquired habits of performance.

Infants are adorable messy little bundles of possibility, and which possibilities become realized and embodied over time depends to a large extent on the nature of the actions that a given individual learns to perform. If the innate predispositions of a given infant are fundamentally incompatible with the demands of neuronormative performance, such that a life of comfortably and convincingly performing neuronormativity isn't within that infant's scope of future possibilities, then we can legitimately say that the infant is neurodivergent—i.e., it has already diverged from the path of neuronormativity, right at the outset.

The reverse, however, doesn't hold true. If the innate predispositions of a given infant *are* compatible with the demands of neuronormative performance, such that neurotypicality *is* within that infant's scope of future possibilities, that's not the same as the infant actually *being* neurotypical yet or being biologically destined for neurotypicality. To say that an infant is innately and "naturally" neurotypical just because it's capable of acclimating to a life of neuronormative performance makes no more sense than saying that the infant is innately and "naturally" a software engineer just because it would be possible to someday teach it to design software.

In other words, it's possible to be born neurodivergent but it's not possible to be born neurotypical. Neurotypicality is a socially instilled mode of normative performance, and is no more innate than the performance of a heteronormative gender role. And like heteronormative gender performance, neurotypicality can be queered; one can subvert the performance and liberate the bodymind (and liberate relationships, activities, spaces, and ultimately cultures) from the constraints of normativity. From a neuroqueer perspective, this is excellent news; it means that no one is biologically doomed to a life of being normal.

Neuroqueer Theory into Neuroqueer Practice

Let's ground this discussion of Neuroqueer Theory in an example of neuroqueer practice. Please note, however, that due to the boundless and heterogeneous scope of neuroqueer possibility, there are innumerable other potential forms of neuroqueer practice that bear no resemblance whatsoever to the example offered here. This example is intended to suggest just one possible avenue of neuroqueer exploration out of a disparate infinitude of potential avenues.

The example I'd like to offer concerns the movement of hands. I choose to focus on hand movement because it's an example in which the overlap of neuronormativity and heteronormativity is particularly evident, and because it's the same example I was contemplating and writing about at the precise moment in 2008 when the term neuroqueer first occurred to me.

The policing of bodies and of embodiment is central to both neuronormativity and heteronormativity, and this includes the policing of how people move their hands. The policing of hands has in fact long played a particularly significant role in the enforcement of neuronormative embodiment. Autistic people have an innate proclivity for using their hands to stim; this stimming can take a wide variety of forms which violate the rules of normative performance to varying degrees (e.g., hands flapping, hands dancing in the air like tree branches in the wind, twisty movements of the fingers tracing patterns in space, hands or fingers rubbing together, hands or fingers exploring or stroking or tapping upon surfaces).

Applied Behavior Analysis (ABA), an abusive and trauma-inducing form of conversion "therapy" aimed at forcing neurodivergent children into compliance with normative performance, seeks among other things to coerce its young victims into suppressing their capacity to stim. Perpetrators of ABA often focus a great deal—creepily and sometimes downright obsessively—on control of their victims' hands, and on the suppression of hand-related stimming in particular. The use of the command "Quiet hands!" by ABA practitioners in this context has led to the adoption of the phrase "loud hands" as one of the slogans of autistic liberation (my first published essay on the neurodiversity paradigm, "Throw Away the Master's Tools," originally appeared in an anthology of autistic activist writings called *Loud Hands*). In the war to subjugate neurodivergent bodyminds, and in neuroqueer resistances to that subjugation, our hands have thus become contested territories of particular importance on both the physical and symbolic levels.

The entwined nature of neuronormativity and heteronormativity means that the compulsory performance of neurotypicality is never a gender-neutral performance, but instead is strongly tied to the performance of binary heteronormative gender roles. Normative performance of whichever gender one was assigned at birth is central to what it means to be "normal" in the eyes of the present dominant culture. Thus, when the enforcers of normativity demand that a child "act normal," it's ultimately a demand to either act like a "normal boy" or like a "normal girl," whether or not the demand is explicitly phrased that way.

Since normative performance is always gendered, deviations from neuronormative embodiment are also inevitably deviations from heteronormative embodiment. Whether a given deviation gets interpreted by the enforcers of normativity as a violation of neuronormativity or as a violation of heteronormativity often depends entirely on context and circumstances. In a context in which a child is known to be autistic (or neurodivergent in some other specific and culturally pathologized way), the child's non-normative usage of their hands is likely to be pathologized as a "symptom" of their neurodivergence. But in a different context, in which those who are policing the child's embodiment are unaware of the child's neurodivergence, the same non-normative hand movements might be flagged as gender violations: children whom adults have labeled as girls might be reprimanded for drumming on the table with their hands or running their fingers vigorously and repeatedly through their hair, on the grounds that such actions are "unladylike"; children whom adults have labeled as boys might be attacked or ridiculed for flapping their hands, on the grounds that such gestures are "gay."

Thus, there are some autistic people who were forced in childhood to suppress their natural hand movements because those hand movements were flagged as "symptoms of autism" and targeted for elimination by autistiphobic adults, and other autistic people who weren't recognized as autistic in childhood but were still forced to suppress their hand movements because those hand movements were violations of heteronormativity that got them targeted for homophobic and transphobic abuse by adults and/or peers. And of course, there are many who were targeted on both neuronormative and heteronormative grounds at different times—e.g., autistics who in their youth were abused by adults for moving their hands autistically, and by homophobic peers who read those same hand movements as queer. The professional ABA perpetrator and the homophobic schoolyard bully are ultimately in the same line of work, enforcing the same compulsory normativity from different angles.

Since distinctively autistic movements of the hands violate the rules of both neuronormative performance and heteronormative performance, to refuse to suppress such movements functions as a

simultaneous queering of both neuronormativity and heteronormativity. When an autistic person chooses to allow themselves to follow
some or all of the impulses toward non-normative hand movement
that spontaneously arise in them, rather than suppressing those impulses in the interest of normative performance, that's a form of neuroqueering.

One can deepen and extend this form of neuroqueering further by
actively working to rediscover, explore, reclaim, and cultivate modes
of non-normative hand movement which one has been suppressing
for so long that the suppression has become ingrained unconscious
habit. There's a growing body of published work, including both
personal accounts and scholarly research, on how the suppression of
non-normative embodiments for the sake of compliance with standards of neuronormative performance (a compliance toward which
the neurodivergent are relentlessly pressured throughout their lives)
does profound psychological harm to neurodivergent people and is
strongly correlated with depression and suicidality. The dominant
culture, in other words, pushes neurodivergent people to prioritize
passing for "normal" at the expense of their own well-being, mirror-
ing the way that queer people have traditionally been pressured to
stay closeted. In the emerging discourse on this issue, the suppression of non-neuronormative embodiments is commonly referred to
as *masking*, and the reclaiming of those embodiments is referred to
as *unmasking*. So it would be entirely accurate to say that neurodivergent unmasking is a form of neuroqueering (one of the most vital
forms, I'd argue).

The sort of bodily unmasking I'm talking about here, the reclaiming of previously suppressed ways of moving, can be intense
and profoundly transformative. When the suppression has become
ingrained unconscious habit (as happens especially when such sup-

pression begins in childhood), it's maintained in large part by the layers of deep, chronic, unconscious muscular tension which Wilhelm Reich referred to as *character armor*. Character armor is the bodily component of repression; it serves not only to block the spontaneous performance of various bodily movements and self-expressions, but also to block access to the feelings, yearnings, organismic impulses, and psychological capacities associated with those movements and self-expressions. The process of recovering one's capacity for spontaneous neuroqueer movement is thus deeply and inseparably entwined with both the process of liberating oneself from the chronic tensions of character armor, and the process of recovering and cultivating modes of self-attunement and embodied expression from which one had previously been cut off by those tensions.

The neuroqueer project of reclaiming specific hand movements and stims that one was forced to suppress in childhood is a doorway to broader vistas of neuroqueer practice: in working to reconnect with those movements, one is also reconnecting with and cultivating one's attunement to the inner stirrings, inclinations, and impulses from which such movements emerge. The cultivation of this attunement can develop over time into a vastly expanded repertoire of spontaneous self-expression and a greater capacity to creatively reshape ourselves. Neuroqueering at its best is not only a creative defiance and subversion of both neuronormativity and heteronormativity, but also simultaneously a path toward living more authentically and creatively than the strictures of normative performance would allow.

Although I've been focusing on autistic hand movements in this discussion, it's equally applicable to the hand movements of any non-autistic neurodivergent folks who might have natural inclinations toward using their hands in distinctive ways that violate the rules of normative performance (and obviously, it's also applicable to aspects of embodiment that have little or nothing to do with hands; I've just chosen to focus on hand movements as an example). Now here's a crucial point: it's also applicable to the hand movements of folks who aren't innately neurodivergent.

Autistics and other innately neurodivergent folks tend to have strong natural proclivities for modes of embodiment (often including ways of using the hands) that violate the rules of normative performance. But the reverse doesn't hold true: neurotypical people aren't born naturally compliant with the rules of normative performance; they're just people who've deeply internalized those rules and are capable of maintaining that performance and *experiencing* it as natural. This doesn't mean that a life spent in the embodied performance of neuronormativity is inevitable or truly natural for them, or that such a life is optimal for their well-being.

For years, in my various public speaking engagements, I've talked to audiences about autistic ways of moving and how being able to freely embody the spontaneous dance of stimming is essential to autistic well-being. In the early days of my public speaking career, when I spoke of the harm that results from the suppression of stimming, and the importance of recovering the capacity to stim and defending the right to have "loud hands," I spoke of these things solely as issues facing the autistic community.

Over time, I started hearing from people who'd been in my audiences at one time or another. They'd contact me to thank me for inspiring them to liberate themselves from the strictures of normative embodiment and reclaim their capacity to stim. They'd tell me that learning to attune to their long-suppressed stimming impulses had expanded their consciousness, sparked interesting changes in their cognitive processes, and helped to restore their joy and vitality and creativity.

What came as a surprise to me was that some of the people who contacted me to tell me these things also told me that they weren't autistic, and that as far as they knew they hadn't started out as innately neurodivergent in any way. Instead, inspired by my words on the topic, they'd diverged from normativity of their own accord, through an intentional reclaiming and exploration of ways of moving and engaging with the sensory world that had lain buried under a socially-instilled shell of neurotypicality since their early childhoods. They'd neuroqueered themselves, and their minds and lives were weirder and better for it.

All babies and toddlers stim. The people we describe as neurotypical tend to lose touch with the capacity for spontaneous stimmy movement as it becomes buried beneath the socially instilled and internalized performance of normative embodiment. Many autistic or otherwise innately neurodivergent people, on the other hand, tend to remain connected to that capacity to whatever extent they manage to resist being shamed and/or brutalized and/or abusively therapized out of their attunement to it. Either way, though, a unique and beautiful version of the spontaneous organismic dance of stimming abides within each and every human being, no matter how deeply repressed it might be in some cases. With sufficient commitment, a proper spirit of open-minded exploration, and a willingness to let go of normal, *anyone* can learn to reconnect with that dance and embody it—and that process of reconnection can start with something as simple as experimenting with using one's hands to stim more.

We are embodied psyches, bodyminds. The organization and processes of the psyche are inextricably entwined with the organization and processes of the body in a single complex system and in a continuous dance of mutual shaping. New ways of moving and using the body create new neural pathways and bring new potentials of consciousness into manifestation. To liberate the body from the in-grained habits, tensions, and inhibitions that keep one locked into the performance of normativity, and to reawaken and cultivate the capacity for spontaneous stimming and non-normative self-embodi-ments, can also serve to help free the mind from the limits of norma-tive perception and cognition.

All queering (including neuroqueering) is inherently transgres-sive, since by definition it involves subverting, defying, deviating from, and/or fucking with normativity. Neuroqueer Theory is thus in some fundamental way oppositional and defiant by its very nature. At the same time, though, it's also radically optimistic in its view that with sufficient engagement in neuroqueer practice, *anyone* can liber-ate themselves from the strictures of normativity. The already neu-rodivergent can reconnect with and cultivate previously suppressed or undeveloped capacities, in order to more fully manifest their po-tentials for beautiful weirdness, and those whom we call neurotypi-cals are just potential neuroqueer mutant comrades who haven't yet woken up and figured out how to unzip their normal-person suits.

I've chosen to build this discussion of neuroqueer practice around a single example, the queering of hand movements. As I noted earli-er, however, there are innumerable possible forms of neuroqueering which, apart from constituting some form of subversion of norma-tivity, have little in common with this particular example. One can neuroqueer any aspect of one's self-embodiment, and one can also neuroqueer art, literature, spaces, systems, fields of academic study, and all manner of other realms of activity.

Neuroqueering on an individual level, in the form of creative bodily enactments that subvert the norms of normative performance and disrupt internalized habits of normative embodiment, serves to materialize previously unrealized neurocognitive and creative potentials. With this awakening of new neuroqueer creative capacities comes an increased capacity to participate in the neuroqueering of cultural spaces and cultural practices: the ongoing co-creation of social environments that support the creative participation of neuroqueer bodyminds and encourage further embodied exploration of neuroqueer performance and neuroqueer possibilities. This sort of ongoing interplay between the neuroqueering of individual bodyminds and the neuroqueering of cultural spaces is the key to collective liberation from compulsory normativity.

Neuronormativity and heteronormativity, in essence, are systems of artificial restriction on human potential. By their very nature, they limit our possibilities. To neuroqueer is to refuse to be constrained by those limits. Wherever restrictive conventions of compulsory neuronormativity and heteronormativity exist, there also exists the potential to open new vistas of creative possibility by queering those conventions in some way or another. The possible forms and horizons of neuroqueer practice are effectively infinite; the amount of space outside of a closet, after all, is always infinitely greater than the amount of space inside the closet.

Acknowledgements

This book wouldn't be what it is without the support of my beloved fellow members of the Autonomous Press collective: B. Martin Allen, Casandra Johns, Andrew M. Reichart, Phil Smith, and Azzia Walker. In particular, Casandra is responsible for making the book look as good as it does, and Andrew went above and beyond in swiftly guiding it through the publication process.

Azzia Walker, the love of my life, supported and encouraged my writing every step of the way, and also kept me alive by making sure that I occasionally stepped away from the computer for exercise and snuggles.

Kris Brandenburger taught me how to use the medium of the essay to explore and communicate my thoughts, back when she was one of my teachers in my undergrad years. Later, as chair of the undergraduate Psychology program at California Institute of Integral Studies, Kris hired me to teach the Neurodiversity Studies course for which I was inspired to create this book as an introductory text.

Some of the ideas in the newer pieces were originally stirred up in my mind by two interviews conducted with me in 2020: a written interview conducted by Dora M. Raymaker (published under the title "Toward a Neuroqueer Future" in the journal *Autism in*

Adulthood in 2021) and a livestreamed video interview conducted by Chloe Farahar and Harry Thompson of Aucademy.

My students at California Institute of Integral Studies have asked me countless intriguing questions over the past decade, and many of the thoughts that ended up in the book were thoughts I first articulated in answer to those questions.

And finally, Ian J. Grand was the professor and mentor in whose graduate Psychodynamics course I was first inspired to coin the term *neuroqueer*. Ian's passed on now to whatever lies beyond this world, but my writing process is still informed by the habit of trying to express each idea in a way that he would have enjoyed reading.

Made in the USA
Coppell, TX
21 August 2024

36320305R00114